The Architect, the Cook and Good Taste

Petra Hagen Hodgson
Rolf Toyka

The Architect, the Cook and Good Taste

On behalf of the Academy of the Hesse Chamber of Architects
and Town Planners

Birkhäuser
Basel · Boston · Berlin

This book has been kindly supported by Gaggenau BSH Appliances Ltd.

Concept and Copy Editing
Petra Hagen Hodgson, Königstein (supervision)
Rolf Toyka, Wiesbaden

Translation
Michael Robinson, London
(other than the contributions of Peter Davey, Ian Ritchie and Claudio Silvestrin)

Graphic Design
Studio Joachim Mildner, Düsseldorf / Zürich
Lithography
farbo Print + Media, Cologne

This book is also available in a German language edition:
ISBN-13: 978-3-7643-7331-3
ISBN-10: 3-7643-7331-8

Bibliographic information published by the Deutsche Nationalbibliothek
The Deutsche Nationalbibliothek lists this publication in the Deutsche Nationalbibliografie;
detailed bibliographic data is available in the Internet at <http://dnb.ddb.de>.

Library of Congress Control Number: 2007922265

© 2007 Birkhäuser Verlag AG
Basel · Boston · Berlin
P.O. Box 133, CH-4010 Basel, Switzerland
Part of Springer Science+Business Media
Printed on acid-free paper produced from chlorine-free pulp. TCF ∞

Printed in Germany

ISBN-13: 978-3-7643-7621-5
ISBN-10: 3-7643-7621-X

9 8 7 6 5 4 3 2 1
www.birkhauser.ch

Contents

Foreword
Barbara Ettinger-Brinckmann/Rolf Toyka

Tradition means handing on the fire, not worshipping the ashes
(Gustav Mahler)

Just as the contents of our refrigerators are an image of globalisation, the architectural garb of the built environment all over the world is becoming increasingly uniform. But is product quality keeping up with this? One bad piece of cooking means one bad meal – so long as there is no damage to health with devastating consequences. But buildings last longer, shaping the place we live in, our villages, towns and regions, over the centuries. So the quality of the built environment is all the more important, and not just functionally and structurally, but aesthetically as well. There have been many complaints about our "inhospitable cities." It all starts with a single badly designed building. Architecture represents an important part of our culture. The Hesse Chamber of Architects and Town Planners and the academy attached to it have been campaigning for a greater awareness of quality for years, and constantly stress that the act of building must of course consider commercial and functional requirements, but above all it has to make a contribution to building culture.

Knowledge and sensitivity are needed if quality is to be insisted upon. We live in a highly specialised world. It calls for joined-up thinking and intellectual exchange between different disciplines to arrive at new viewpoints. So for ten years now the basic work of the Hesse Chamber of Architects and Town Planners has included addressing interfaces with other culture spheres intensively. Subjects included "architecture and music," "architecture and literature," "architecture and film" and "architecture and theatre." So the idea for this book has its origins in an interdisciplinary symposium on "architecture and culinary culture" organised by the academy of the Hesse Chamber of Architects and Town Planners in cooperation with the *Deutsches Architekturmuseum*, under the direction of Petra Hagen Hodgson and Rolf Toyka. This revealed fundamental links and parallels between the two art forms. These first insights gained at the symposium have been condensed into this volume of texts, now with additional, more detailed lines of thought.

Cooking lab

Why is it that the subject of links between architecture and cooking should seem particularly worth studying? Both arts are essential "staffs of life." If we start addressing the question of quality, then in the case of both cooking and building we see that quality does not have to be associated with high costs. On the contrary, it is about devising intelligent, creative solutions using basic ingredients or materials – and these can be very simple. Some critics have asked in the context of the symposium whether there are not more urgent problems than pursuing ideas about building and cooking. There is no doubt that the current economic situation has to be seen as difficult. But this does not make cultural demands – whether they are aesthetic or ethical – any less significant. On the contrary, if efficiency is the only goal considered, along with cost and questions of short-term gain, there is a danger that we shall lose culture altogether. It is much more that it is a special challenge to aspire, committedly and creatively, to cultural achievements that "pay" in the long term, despite constraining circumstances. True art is not exclusive or elitist, one of its values includes "moderation" – in the way we treat our resources, our space, our aesthetic means. Today things that are fashionable, shrill and exalted tend to be unduly highly rated in architecture, in order to stand out from the masses. Juhani Pallasmaa had some hard words to say about the general trend towards this ego-related architecture at the symposium on "architecture and perception" in Frankfurt am Main (2002): "Most buildings that have been praised in the international press in recent years are characterized by narcissism and nihilism. It is time for this hegemony of the visual to be broken at last in favour of re-sensualising, re-eroticising and re-enchanting the world. Here architecture has the role of restoring the inner world. Instead of experiencing the fact that we are here in the world through architectural space, architecture has deteriorated into the art of the printed image, and has lost its three-dimensional and material quality." Moderation does not mean hankering after publicity and fame, but suggests a carefully considered approach to a given task on the basis of the matter in hand; it means concentrating on essentials. This also includes being aware of tradition and history in particular. Innovative solutions – as in cooking – based on background knowledge are equally desirable for architecture and urban development, landscape architecture and interior design. It is also a matter of making the general public more profoundly able to understand questions about their built environment. One of the many activities that the Chamber has arranged in this context is the annual "Architecture Day." Architecture today is far from most people's everyday thinking and experience, and it is for this reason that an approach to this broad topic is being promoted in schools in particular, under the heading *Architektur macht Schule* – "architecture goes to school" or "architecture becomes the accepted thing." So the Chamber does not simply mount isolated campaigns, but is also responsible for a variety of publications providing pupils and teachers with sound teaching materials. It is important for young children to enjoy looking at their built environment and to acquire criteria and standards for judging architectural quality because today's schoolchildren will be tomorrow's clients and decision-makers, making a considerable contribution (with us) to the shape of the world we live in. Once a sense of quality has been acquired it is possible to resist the above-mentioned architectural shift towards global uniformity, to work against architecture aiming solely at short-term gain and against the compulsion to be spectacular. The Slow Food movement is doing this sort of work in the field of cooking. It now has over 80,000 members world-wide, and is devoted above all to training the sense of taste, and it is also proving successful as a counter-movement to Fast Food, seen as a synonym for Junk Food. In architecture, the efforts being made by institutions including the *Deutsches Architekturmuseum*, the *Architekturmuseum* in Munich, the local architecture centres and the *Baukultur* Foundation. If this book can give further impetus to strengthening a relevant movement for promoting quality architecture with values, a great deal will have been achieved. What this book is not offering: magic solutions for cooking and building. It is much more about passing on the fire Gustav Mahler was talking about – through a future-oriented recollection of tradition.

Architecture workshop

Introduction
Petra Hagen Hodgson

Halfway up the Sacro Monte, near to the town of Varese, was a simple little restaurant. It consisted of just one long, light room with tables with white cloths and high wooden basketwork chairs. The room was built close by the mountainside, light poured into the plain space through the wide-open French windows that made up the longitudinal façade of the building. These French windows connected the room with the terrace, paved with weathered stones and surrounded by stone walls. Two fig trees, lavender shrubs and rosemary bushes were growing on it, and there was a fine view of the Po plain. The owner carried the tables out on to the terrace in fine weather. At Sunday lunchtime families got together here with uncle and aunt, grandma and grandpa round one of the long tables and lingered over their meal until well into the afternoon. The owner was the cook as well, and he often came over to the guests, keen to know how good the food was tasting – but essentially to share the delight he took in his art. The food was always wonderful, even though it was comparatively simply prepared, using the tastiest products of a particular season – spicy tomatoes, deep purple aubergines, fresh, fragrant herbs, the best olive oil, butter and cream from the nearby dairy. The *padrone* cooked and served as though all the guests were part of his family. Sometimes everyone got together round one big table. Guests find that this feeling of human fellowship in an atmosphere defined by the warm-hearted personality of the cook, as manifest in his delicious food, and by the modest but clear, natural spatial situation, remains with them to this day. Many of them have regularly tried to find the same thing again – wherever they may have come from – but have rarely come across anything as naturally right as this.

This book is devoted to exploring how architecture and cooking work together, and thus approaching the question of "good taste": building and cooking are two profoundly human activities with many points of contact. What is it that connects the art of building with the art of cooking? What are the connections based on, and how are the assumed parallels between them expressed? What conclusions can be drawn from a comparison? Above all: how do they actually contribute to our good humour and well-being as human beings? Both building and cooking measure and consider proportion, they impose form and shape, fit together and compose. Aesthetic categories like harmony, proportion and composition, which as a rule are attributed more to architectural design, also apply to cooking. The use of the human body as a yardstick for harmonious proportions is common to both architecture and cuisine. Both are based on the materials i.e. the ingredients used. And more: what is the significance of cooking and building for personal feelings and sensations? And beyond this: what part do they play for us human beings living together? People create "memory archives."[1] Our values, perceptions and (taste) sensations are crucially shaped by our memories of own personal life stories and the collective cultural experience buried deep in our memories of social rituals in earlier days. Marcel Proust called it the "measurable edifice of memory". Ritual, tradition and (taste) memory are part of both building and cooking. How do they affect our thinking today? They are present for us – and not just through architectural

[1] Hartmann, Andreas at the *Deutsches Architekturmuseum* symposium about architecture and perception, November 21st and 22nd 2002 in Frankfurt am Main

tracts and cookery books. How do they affect our action? Architects work with the claim of being specialists in the human aspects of building and design. But cooking is seldom aware that social, psychological and aesthetic factors are part of their activities as well, and that they actively work on them every day. Cooking is able – just like architecture, to report precisely on a culture, a region or a person. So cooking does not just mean preparing appetizing food, but is a cultural activity on the same plane as architectural work – even though it is a more transient art as such.

We have Martin Heidegger to thank indirectly for shedding a key light on the essential connection between building and cooking, which happened when he was reflecting on the connection between building and living.[2] Starting with the common etymological links between the two words in German, he shows that they can be viewed practically identically in the sense of the species-specific "being-on-earth" of us human beings. Put like this, building (*bauen*) includes tilling the earth (*bebauen*), the *cultura*, and creating buildings, both aspects of what was originally also contained in the term *wohnen* (living in the sense of dwelling). *Wohnen* had the additional semantic link with *bleiben*, "staying," and "being pacified," reflecting the aspect of local or home roots. According to Heidegger, human building creates the place, and the place creates the room, the space in which people live, their habitat. When he says "*Bauen* (…) is not only a means and a way to *wohnen*, *bauen* is itself already *wohnen*,"[3] it is then clear that that *wohnen* is more all-embracing, implying a basic human need, the need for one's own centre, a mid-point for one's own world. Vilém Flusser characterises this need as follows: "We dwell. We could not live if we did not dwell. We would be unhoused and unprotected. Exposed to a world without a centre. Our dwelling is the middle of the world. We thrust out into the world from it, and then return to it. We challenge the world from our dwelling, and we take refuge from the world in our dwelling. The world is the surroundings of our dwelling. It is our dwelling that fixes the world. Traffic between dwelling and world is life."[4] These anthropological reflections by Heidegger and Flusser reveal the essential relationship of building and cooking: the latter is one of the elemental cultural activities of dwelling that contribute to consolidating the human "centre." Where other than in the kitchen or at the dining table does family, social life crystallise most closely, thus contributing to the emotional and social establishment of a human home or centre?[5] The ideas put forward in this book group themselves, pictorially speaking, around this dining table – the laid table symbolising the "centre" of life.

[2] Cf. Heidegger, Martin: Bauen Wohnen Denken. In: Otto Bartning (ed): Mensch und Raum. Darmstädter Gespräch 1951, Darmstadt, 1951, pp. 72-84

[3] Ibid. p. 73

[4] Flusser, Vilém quoted from: Botta, Mario: Architektur und Gedächtnis. Wege zur Architektur 2, Brakel, 2005

[5] Despite opinions to the contrary, the meal prepared for the domestic dining table is mainly still eaten communally. Cf. Leimgruber, Walter: Adieu Zmittag. In NZZ Folio pp.16-23, 6/2006

9

Café-restaurant in Aachen

Anatol Herzfeld: Parliament, Hombroich Museum Island 2005

[6] Cf. for table placings: Zischka, Ulrike; Ottomeyer, Hans; Bäumler, Susanne (eds.): Die anständige Lust. Von Esskultur und Tafelsitten, Munich, 1994, p. 138. Of course there were not just "round tables", but above all centrally ordered hierarchies at rectangular tables, or tables placed together in a U-shape, or people arranged themselves as they wished – according to the social order within the community that the table placings were intended to express.

[7] Cf. Endermann, Heinz (adapt.): So du zu Tische wollest gan. Tischzuchten aus acht Jahrhunderten, Berlin, 1991, p. 141

[8] Cf. Elias, Norbert: The Civilizing Process. Oxford, 2000 (2nd edition)

[9] Right down to the "tyranny of intimacy", Cf. Sennett, Richard: The Fall of Public Man. New York 1976. This is only apparently contradicted by what Terence Riley called the "The Un-Private House" (exhibition of the same name at the Museum of Modern Art, New York) or what the Deutsches Architekturmuseum catalogue on the revision of Postmodernism showed in 2003 under the general heading "Life Without Nostalgia" about all Foba Architects' "Aura" house in Tokyo, which manages without a bathroom and with a very small kitchen with a washbasin and refrigerator. These urban nomads have to go to the nearby restaurant to eat and to the public baths to bathe.

[10] Weiss, Richard: Häuser und Landschaften der Schweiz. Zurich, 1959, p. 101

[11] Weiss, Richard: Volkskunde der Schweiz. Zurich, 1946, pp.98/99

[12] Cf. Aicher, Otl's book: Die Küche zum Kochen. Das Ende einer Architekturdoktrin, Munich, 1982

We do not just assuage our hunger at table, hunger drives people to take food in order to survive. This is where they develop their ability to participate in human society. Immanuel Kant was aware of this meaning when he invited people to join him at home for a communal midday meal. King Arthur's round table, around which everyone sat on an equal footing, is still the ancestor of "round tables" as an expression for a community with equal rights.[6] Many versions of table manners and table placings developed over the millennia confirm the central significance of taking food communally for human beings. It was no coincidence that the sociologist Norbert Elias chose human table customs for his study "The Civilizing Process", in order to demonstrate the general civilisation process using changing social standards like forbidding belching at the table, or the introduction of polite eating with a knife and fork. Elias explains the emergence of the embarrassment threshold and the boundary of shame[7] by explaining that changing circumstances are not just something that creeps up on people from the outside, as it were: "The circumstances that change are the relations between the people themselves."[8] And finally he also uses it to describe the story of increasing human privacy and individualisation,[9] for which architecture provides the appropriate spatial framework.

The Roman architectural theorist Vitruvius explained to us in detail that the fire and the roof were the most primordial and essential conditions of domesticity. The house, as a third skin, protects people from the inclemency of the weather, sheltering them from wind, rain and other dangers. Fire provides warmth, light and homely comfort. It was the sacrificial precinct, the workplace, and made and still makes it possible to cook and preserve foodstuffs. A settled existence and ultimately urbanisation could develop only once it became possible to conserve and store food. As Richard Weiss shows in his study of buildings and landscapes in Switzerland, owning one's own, precious fire and thus one's own smoke even became "the legal condition for full mark-community rights in the country and civic majority in the town. (…) So a fire of one's own is not just a sign of domesticity in old law, but actually a real prerequisite for enjoying the mark-community rights and duties"[10] of a citizen. As building technology progressed, and housing was rationalised and differentiated from the single-room house to the "living apparatus, with many rooms, specialised for a whole range of purposes, which largely divided and dissolved the natural domestic community, and also the family,"[11] the "primeval fire" shifted into the background. We have efforts in the 1920s to thank for Befreites Wohnen ("Liberated Living"), the title of a little book dated 1929 by Sigfried Giedion, intended to express the idea of a new life in an open, democratic society, the free ground plan, fluid space, but also the large extent to which our living spaces have been functionalised, with the kitchen downgraded as a merely functional cooking lab. At the same time, cooking was rationalised and functionalised, tailored to the professional woman, and embodied in fast food prefabricated production from tins or the freezer. When the kitchen – understood as the central (living-) space of the house – is reduced to a rationalised, technical laboratory, a merely functional space, where almost everything can be done at the touch of a button, this does not do justice to the importance and meaning ascribed to the kitchen, since it disregards the psychological sense of being housed (and cooked for). It may be fashionable today to arrange the kitchen and with it the dining room as an accessory in the spirit of modern ideas about lifestyle,[12] but this fails to acknowledge its role as a space that creates meaning.

Bakehouse, still in use, in the centre of Salouf, the Grisons

Bread cooling in the Salouf bakehouse

To comply with fire regulations, the working bread oven in this 1637 house thrusts out through the outside wall. Mons, the Grisons

But kitchens are not the only architectural spaces in our cities and countryside to give shape to the activity of preparing and storing food, and this does not just mean the grain silos, slaughterhouses and cast-iron market halls that provided structural and formal models for architects in the 1920s, it also includes bakeries, for example: this is where something that is possibly the most important foodstuff for many peoples[13] was and is made: bread. Even heat from all sides is needed to bake bread. In Western Europe, people went on cooking at an open fire or open hotplate for a long time. If the heating stove with the appropriate additional equipment could not meet the needs of baking, a special oven was installed in the kitchen, or people set up their own bakehouse, usually meeting the needs of several families. The people of the Grisons village of Salouf, near Savognin, still bake their bread in a communal bakehouse of this kind. It is directly on the main village square, never noticed by tourists, and forms part of the village community's public life.

If questions are asked about criteria for the quality of buildings or foods, the matter of good taste inevitably crops up. What exactly is taste? It is – like the "home memory" that we carry in us – a sense of memory, a sense based on memories and sensations. It helps us to explore the qualities of things. Taste is first of all the physical ability to taste, a sensual pleasure or – according to Immanuel Kant, who has left us a wonderfully lucidly fashioned treatise about taste in his writings on anthropology[14] – the *Wohlgeschmack* (pleasant taste) that also implies enjoyment. The Middle High German word *gesmac* is indeed a borrowed form of the Italian word *gusto* or Latin *gustare*, which suggests tasting and enjoying at the same time. For Kant, *Wohlgeschmack* is a subjective value judgement. But at the same time, following Kant, taste suggests a general ability to distinguish (whether something is sweet or savoury, sour or bitter), an ability to distinguish acquired by experience and agreement, and, as a third category, the ability to make generally valid judgements.[15] So Kant defines taste as "the ability of aesthetic judgement to choose in a way that is generally valid. Thus it is an ability to make social judgements of outside objects in the imagination."[16] This aesthetic judgement depends on shared values in society, i.e. judgements relating to taste are always about the society's values. In other words, pure, sensual enjoyment of what there is on my plate, for example, and the way I judge it depends on ideas about value that are shared with other people. According to Kant, good taste is socially determined.[17] Hence common experience – and this was the situation in the Sacro Monte restaurant – makes enjoyment greater, even more valuable. Because man has individual creative intelligence a priori, making him free to decide, we do not all judge in the same way – unless we are indulging in mere imitation. It is then that a judgement of taste becomes a fashion. For Kant, the criterion for good taste is moderation; finding moderation leads to morality. Hence he argues that "ideal taste tends towards the outward promotion of morality,"[18] not merely pursuing pleasure, but with a higher aim. Thus there is an ethical and moral component inherent in true value judgement. This is explicitly present in the three Slow Food[19] categories "good" (biologically valuable and sensual), "clean" (ecologically sustainable) and "just" (ethically sustainable). Vitruvius's categories *utilitas* (usefulness), *firmitas* (solidity) and *venustas* (gracefulness) can be interpreted similarly in today's language. So good taste – as a moral and ethical category – should above all make allies of the architect and the cook. For cooking and building touch upon profoundly social questions.

[13] Paczensky, Gert von; Dünnebier, Anna: Kulturgeschichte des Essens und Trinkens. 77 ff. Even the ancient Egyptians ate bread. When it was in short supply, this led to grain riots or the plundering of bakeries. The grain laws of 123 BC were passed in Ancient Rome at the time of the Republic, conceding that every citizen, whether poor or rich and independently of his social status, was entitled to bread free of charge. There was a comparable decree at the time of the French Revolution, which went further, and prescribed that everyone should have the same bread.

[14] Kant, Immanuel: Schriften zur Anthropologie, Geschichtsphilosophie, Politik und Pädagogik. Wilhelm Weischedel (Hg.), Werke in zehn Bänden, Darmstadt, Sonderausgabe, 1983. p. 563-579; full English text in: Kant, Immanuel: Anthropology from a Pragmatic Point of View, transl. by Mary J. Gregor, The Hague 1974.

[15] If for Kant reason was the authority that leads to general validity, today we would say that it is common value judgements that provides that which can be generalised in the judgement of taste.

[16] Translated by Michael Robinson; original German text: „das Vermögen der ästhetischen Urteilskraft, allgemein gültig zu wählen. Er [der Geschmack] ist also ein Vermögen der gesellschaftlichen Beurteilung äußerer Gegenstände in der Einbildungskraft. ibid p. 565.

[17] See ibid. p. 570.

[18] Translated by Michael Robinson; oiginal German text: daß „...der ideale Geschmack eine Tendenz zur äußeren Beförderung der Moralität" hat... ibd p. 570.

[19] The movement promotes healthy eating using high-quality, tasty foodstuffs that are essential for human well-being. At the same time it resists the standardisation that is threatened everywhere and encourages biodiversity, and also ecologically and socially acceptable production methods. One of the Slow Food movement's major interests is training the sense of taste. Cf. Petrini, Carlo: Slow Food. Genießen mit Verstand. Zurich, 2003 and the article in this book.

In this book, the artist and "lateral thinker" Peter Kubelka writes about the need to think about the "unity of all things" again and identifies cultural links with the early days of our culture. As an ethnologist, Andreas Hartmann familiarises us with the theme of human connections with the past. Gion Caminada's work takes an architectural approach that demonstrates how a building tradition developed over centuries – the "knitted building" in this case – can be translated into meaningful contemporary form and developed further. The artist Onno Faller, who pursues cooking as an art genre, describes a classical Swabian sequence of dishes that is still cooked on peasant occasions today. The order of the dishes is by no means random, but thoroughly structured, coherent in itself, following centuries-old ways of preparing the food determined by the evolution of the dish and also by laws for the sensual perception of three-dimensional objects. The architecture theorist Fritz Neumeyer writes above all about the social aspects linking the art of building and the art of cooking. The architecture critic Peter Davey explains the connection between fire, hearth and home in his account of the historical development of the kitchen. Then the architect and author Wilhelm Klauser presents the history of restaurant development. The Panetteria in Milan, designed by Claudio Silvestrin, lies behind the great importance that bread still has today as a basic food – expressed in architecture reduced to essentials. Stanislaus von Moos's contribution examines the pictorial language of food in architectural discourse from an art-historical angle, showing how amazingly frequently the pictorial language of food is used in architectural discourse. The art historian Paul von Naredi-Rainer casts light on the connections between dimension and number, proportion and harmony in architecture, Renate Breuß, who has examined historical recipe material as an art historian, considers these aspects from a culinary perspective. The architect Annette Gigon answers questions about thinking in terms of proportions and numerical ratios in contemporary architecture. But above all – like the cook Raymond Blanc talking about the ingredients he uses – she discusses the importance of materials in architectural design. The Slow Food movement is also concerned about the quality of materials: it started about 20 years ago in Italy, based on the conviction that mass production guided by productivity and quantity destroys the environment, traditions and ways of life. By asking questions about quality criteria for foodstuffs, Slow Food – as Carlo Petrini, its president, writes –, trains people in good taste. The architectural theoretician Ákós Moravánszky discusses whether taste can be reproduced, while the food chemist Udo Pollmer broaches the issue of globalisation and with it a consumerist orientated levelling of taste that can equally be noticed in architecture. And finally the architect Ian Ritchie introduces an architecture based on ecological responsibility, wanting to do justice to ethical slow food criteria in the search for sustainable solutions.

Theo Dannecker: Still Life with Tomatoes 1998

Architecture and Food Composition
Peter Kubelka

Cuisine now generally suggests something exquisite, special, out of the ordinary. But what about noodle soup? Noodle soup, which is a hundred times more important than the dab of kiwi foam topping the creations of so-called "haute" cuisine. Food today has detached itself from wellbeing. What is seen as the art of cooking serves the eye first and foremost. It has retreated to gigantic plates with a single pea in the middle, on a bed of some tasteless foam. Prospects are bad for the starred chef, who cooks for an international public that doesn't want to put on weight and eats for the sake of prestige. All that is left for him is compromises verging on the innocuous, starting with the ingredients. The result is the blandness of easy digestibility, without crusts and layers of fat, without any characteristic flavour. And it is the "starred cooks" who mask these dreary tastes with visual tricks, with red, green and carved vegetables. So all the eater can do is distance himself from his senses. They become dulled.

But what is cooking really? And what is the connection with architecture? Preparing food means constructing food, assembling, composing. The process of constructing food is similar to architecture. I should like to pull back a little further to explain the close link between cooking and architecture. I think that everyone – not just architects and cooks – needs to think back to the unity of everything that was once the case. We must understand again that all our deeds and thoughts – and that includes cooking and building – are permeated with the ancient past, and with tradition.

Nepalese water vessels

One example might illustrate this. If early man wanted a drink, he had to find a spring and go to it. He had to bend down humbly, kneel, hollow his hand and drink the water from this hollow hand, water that the mountain had kept ready for him over thousands of years. In the course of his long development, man learned to construct this mountain for himself – in the form of a water-bottle. Ultimately it is nothing more than a carved out hollow, proportioned so that it can be held comfortably in the hand, with the water in it. And just as for food preparation, architects have to deal with hollows. Actually the architect should not be called "architectus" but "archicavus." The fact is that architects are hollowers, hollowers out. But the hollows are modelled on nature – using our own bodies. We are surrounded by hollows. Even a dog turning round in a circle, scratching at the ground and then lying down in the hollow it has created is working as an architect: it is hollowing out, creating a comfortable space for itself.

Stone house near Perugia

Seen in terms of cultural history, preparing food, supplying people with nourishment, is even older than architecture, which offers protection from rain and cold. This makes it mankind's oldest art form. Like all other artistic disciplines, cooking expresses a civilization's world view. Until 1980, when I was professor at the Städel Art Institute in Frankfurt and started a course on film and cooking, the idea that cooking was an art was totally alien. Cooking and architecture – both functional activities – existed long before cave painting. Cooking is the mother of philosophy, of chemistry, of physics. Cooking is poetry, is transformation. While painting – which can be used only to look at – is scarcely more than 40,000 years old, preparing food goes back millions of years. This can be illustrated by the common origins of tools and art. All the arts once came into being as necessary tools for a specific purpose. Tools are used for working on material things. Art serves to work on something intangible and bring it vividly to life. But the starting point of every art is the *objet trouvé*, the existing material, in other words, something that makes

Circular single-room house with farmland, Nepal

people think of certain things. We know the *objet trouvé* from Modern art, and also from our own lives. I grew up in the country, and as a youth I often used to sit in the evenings with my friend Franzi by a little fire we had baked stolen potatoes in. We were hunters and gatherers. We had acquired the potatoes from a nearby field, and then put them into the fire. The cows were quiet. So we sat there and enjoyed this precious commodity – leisure. And so you think about things, look around for no particular reason and see a cloud. Until Franzi said: "Hey, it looks like a horse:" that was the beginning of art, the *objet trouvé*. No one had worked on this cloud, and yet it became a work of art.

15

And that is how the first tools began. The tools we are born with are not very successful in comparison with the animal kingdom. We do not have decent tusks, like wild boars. But we have this magnificent instrument called a hand that we can pick up a stone with. I suggest that it was the hand that made us into men, because it made us into a being that changes its species with every tool. We are transformed when holding an instrument in our hand. At first it was just some stone we had picked

Stonehenge, England

up. Later we found a stone that still had not been changed, but that fitted our hand precisely. Later we found the worked-on stone. It might have been split by a blow that gave it a point and a cutting edge. Adapted stones like this, which were also used for preparing food and creating rooms are over 2.8 million years old. Man took thousands of years before being able to strike a blow of this kind deliberately, to make a tool for himself. And it is just the same with architecture. Pygmies in Central Africa still pick a leaf and use it as an umbrella. This umbrella is one of the first major architectural events. But the leaf can be used in different ways. It can be folded over and used as a hat. At home the pygmies use it as a plate, or as an envelope for a roast. In short: cooking and architecture use tools, they are craft and art at the same time.

Cavities: Central space in Frank Lloyd Wright's Guggenheim Museum rotunda in New York, completed 1959

But back to the hollows. We live in a world made up of a lot of hollows that our senses sample and limit. Man experiences the universe as a hollow with his eyes. The ear reaches as far as the air will carry the vibrations. The nose reaches further than the ear can hear, as far as a paper factory or a bad perfume can stink. But much more important is the vault of what can be grasped, in both senses: what we can physically grasp on the one hand and what can be grasped in the transferred sense. We also experience the world as hollows when we swallow via our mouth. As in architecture, crucial statements are made in cooking through three-dimensional objects. The mouth is an organ that is much better than the eye at analysing spatial situations. In fact we know that stone is hard, that glass is cold and that wood is soft – which in architecture we can read with our eyes – by touching, and not least by touching with the mouth and tongue, which we used in our childhood to feel and lick our way into the world. For example, the mouth does not examine a forkful of pasta from a distance, like the eye. On the contrary, the portion of pasta is directly sampled in the hollow of the mouth, shifted around, chopped up and crushed. The tongue and the palate assess, grasp the form and break it down. The pasta is architecture for the mouth. The mouth provides the brain with precise information about shape, surface, the nature of the material, but also about the smell, taste and temperature of the food that is just being taken apart and chopped up. If the character of the pasta – whether it is penne, farfalle or spaghetti – is to be read by the mouth, it must be "al dente." That means it must be properly cooked and of good quality. The eye may still acknowledge overcooked, mushy noodles as what they are, but the mouth at the latest will unmask them as an indifferent mass.

Discoveries during the development of mankind that have led to new eras manifest themselves in a whole variety of artistic activities – if not always at the same time. A new era dawned for cooking with the invention of pasta. In architecture, something similar happened with the invention of building in brick. The brick has been part of the history of human civilisation ever since prehistoric man started experimenting with dried clay. First of all, man invented bricks made by mixing clay with straw, shaping them into handy cuboids and drying them in the sun. Despite their irregular shape and natural defects they made excellent building material for primitive huts. As the need for different and more complex buildings arose, these clay bricks were no longer adequate. Bricks baked in a kiln had to be invented. By doing this, man had created a valuable new material that made it possible to build much more complicated buildings than simple huts to live in. Building with fired bricks revolutionised the practical possibilities of architecture, and with it the architects' imaginations. Fired bricks are small, hand crafted elements. They are formally repetitive and can be used to create much freer shapes than elements adopted directly from nature like stone blocks or tree trunks. It was only now that the Pantheon could be devised. Roman brick architecture made larger, self-supporting ceiling areas possible, greater spans between massive building sections and more strongly articulated surfaces. The same happened in cooking. Pasta revolutionised the architecture of the mouth. A bite of pasta is made up of small, crafted usually geometrical elements that do not occur in nature. It can convey new experiences of form to the eater that were not possible before with porridge or bread, meat or vegetables.

Pantheon in Rome

18

Modern brickwork art: Mario Botta's Museum of Modern Art in San Francisco, 1990-1995

All Italian pasta tastes more or less the same, as it is always made of the same grano duro. And yet each type has a different consistency, is a different size, a different shape and thus conveys an unmistakable message. One pasta comes from Naples, for example, the other hails from Arezzo. If a Sicilian who has emigrated bends over a plate in New York containing the Sicilian pasta he grew up with that his wife has prepared for him, then he is at home when eating. Then he suddenly knows who he is again and where he comes from. In fact the foods we are brought up with form a crucial part of a person's identity, his home. Like the mother tongue, "mother foods" have a vocabulary that remains stored for a lifetime. That is why it is so tragic when the noodle soup mentioned at the beginning or the traditional roast pork are spurned today. Simple dishes, canonised over the centuries, are true works of art – without claiming to be art.

Architecture originated as a subtractive process. In other words, if there is too much in the hollow, anything superfluous is taken out. If a hollow, or cave, was found in early times, it was probably left just as it was. Or early man had to throw the cave bears out of it. That is a cleansing operation. Or man decided to take away certain heaps of earth, to clean the cave, to enlarge it, to create some space. That is architecture. A photographer works in just the same way – to bring a modern medium into it. First, his camera-cave captures everything the lens has in front of it. Then the photographer's job is to get rid of everything that is not needed in the picture. Painting, on the other hand, is an additive process. The painter starts at zero with a white canvas. What he does not paint on the canvas does not exist. Cooking and architecture mean both: subtracting and adding. Architecture starts with clearing out and then continues with additive accumulation. So the pyramid and the grave mound come into being, and walls and roofs emerge. The same principle is used in cooking.

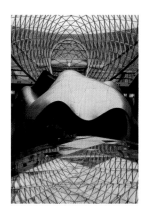

Cave-like interior life in the DG Bank in Berlin, 2001

Additive accumulation: Norman Foster's Reichstag Dome in Berlin, 1995-1999

19

When looking at the processes of food preparation, cooking is actually about allowing things to disintegrate deliberately. Nature shows us how. We just boost the natural cooking process for making air-dried ham by hanging the piece of raw meat on a nail in the open air. If we want to eat a schnitzel, we need various tools to cut the piece of raw meat up. We have to mince the meat, chop it up, beat it. Only then does the great moment of cooking arrive. Now something is added to the meat. This brings us to another key word, the metaphor. Food always conveys a message in the artistic sense, just like architecture, painting, sculpture, poetry or music. The metaphor, as a message-conveying technique, juxtaposes concepts. In cooking edible elements are juxtaposed, in architecture it is the spaces we live in. If we change them, we are signalling a change of identity at the same time. The Austrian bread soup is a complex metaphor going back to the Middle Ages, it is a satisfying soup, a soup with body. It consists of meat, water, bread, egg and sour cream. This soup's uncanny metaphor lies in the marriage of fire and water. When meat is hung over a fire so that the smoke can work on it, the meat drinks in the smoke, as it were, the smoke permeates the meat. Water cannot be smoked. Nevertheless, it takes on the taste of fire from the smoked meat. The solid consistency is created by finely chopped white bread that is cooked to shreds in the "fire-water," and the mouth can detect these, it can read them. Egg is added to the shreds of white bread, and in the soup these mutate into shreds of egg, which feel firmer in the mouth. Sour cream is added as the finishing touch. If it had been put into the soup straight away, it would have split. In this way it creates a milky, uniform liaison. Sour cream is nothing more than thickened milk that is cooked, changed, i.e. fermented as paid labour by the tiny creatures we call bacteria. This gives the milk another flavour component, making it acidic and able to keep for a longer time. Milk is the pinnacle of nourishment, the model for nourishment. Milk alone is enough to keep a child alive. By eating, the mother prepares the nourishment for her baby in her body. Ultimately cooking is a continuation of breast-feeding.

The invention of principles that later changed the world, in literature, philosophy, technology have already been defined through study and the preparation of edible material. Seen in this way, cooking, the preparation of food, is the oldest active change of man's universe. To explain this, another example from my childhood: my mother took me raspberry-picking one day. She knew the fruit, and she knew where to find the raspberry bushes. I put the raspberry I had picked straight into my mouth, like a bird and was happy, but my mother came up with a container – a hollow space that can be carried, offering protection. She taught me to make a cultural leap. When I had picked the next raspberry and was about to eat it, she made me stop. She said: "Cup your hand. Pick a raspberry with the other one but don't eat it, just put it in the hollow of your hand. Pick another raspberry, again, don't eat it. Wait! Put it into the hollow of your hand. Pick another raspberry and again, don't eat it. Keep going till you've filled the hollow of your hand. Now look at the heap of raspberries, smell them and put them all in your mouth." My impatience was rewarded with an event that doesn't happen like that in nature. All the raspberries from one bush condensed into a handful: wonderful! In this way my mother had shown me a concept that mankind discovered with the preparation of food: the concept of condensing energy. This condensation process does not need any tools. It was known to pre-stone-age man. An action as mundane as collecting a handful of strawberries shows how mankind thousands of generations ago started developing insights that now drive technology. We should always keep an eye on our origins. Only by doing so are we able to understand what we are moving towards, faster and faster. Creativity, improvisation and imagination can produce something wonderful only if one works with elements that one knows and if one is able to speak a traditional language.

This essay is based on a two-hour performance given by Peter Kubelka at the "Architecture and Culinary Culture" symposium at Kloster Eberbach near Wiesbaden in March 2004 – condensed by Petra Hagen Hodgson; selection of images also by Petra Hagen Hodgson.

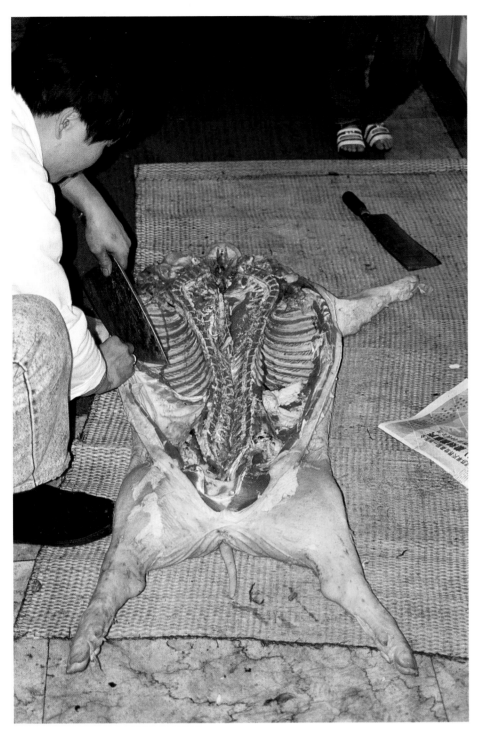

Slaughtering a pig

Measurement and Number in Architecture
Paul von Naredi-Rainer

I

Plato ranked architecture above the arts that exhaust themselves in mere imitation because it is guided not just by intuition, but uses measurements and numbers, and thus is able to create an inner order. Measurement and number are universals in architecture. They are not just essential if it is to be realised technically – from the dimensions of the stone blocks in an ancient house to the metal cladding for the Guggenheim Museum in Bilbao, for which the calculations could be made only by computer –, but also indicators for its aesthetic quality.

The *number* forms the basis for quantitative thinking, which attempts to comprehend and order the relationships between mankind and the world around it. Its range extends from magic ideas, which see the number as a mythical object with ascribed attributes and powers, to scientific thinking, in which the number is a mathematical object as an ideal entity.

Measurement forms the basis of even the most primitive technology. From the earliest days of human culture determining dimensions, above all length, weight and time, has been fundamentally important. Measuring means comparing by using numbers. It means representing a quantity (the measurand or measured variable) in terms of a number (dimension value), which shows how often the base unit of measurement is contained in the quantity to be measured. So it is not possible to measure without number and unit of measurement – and it is not possible to build without measuring.

There is a great deal of variety within the highly nuanced combinations of words that have accumulated around the term *measure* – measured behaviour as opposed to unmeasured behaviour that can lead to immoderation, due measure and lack of measure, and then measurability and loss of measure, "like doth quit like, and Measure still for Measure" – all suggesting that *measure* is central to a broad field of meaning embracing ethics, aesthetics and also natural science. This linguistic connection between spheres that are now separate shows origins in the concept of measure in Greek thinking. This developed a measure that could be applied to man from the equation of the good and the beautiful in the *Kalokagathia*, including ethical and aesthetic, religious, political, physical and psychological matters. This measure is based on a divine order of the universe that is declared to be immutable, with which man must conform in order to be part of that order. We come across this basic idea in Christianity as well. Christ himself speaks of the "temple of his body" (John 2,21), using an image that was current before Christianity and is repeatedly taken up in Christian exegesis. The Church teacher Augustine (354-430) established a connection extending beyond the metaphorical between Christ's human form and the church building: he sees an Old Testament reference to Christ as the redeemer of mankind and a model for the church in the ark that rescued Noah and his family from the great flood. The dimensions of this ark (300 x 50 x 30 ells) symbolise the human body in whose form Christ redeemed the world: "The length of the human body from the top of the head to the sole of the foot is six times the width from one side to another and ten times the depth from back to belly" (de civitate Dei XV/26.1).

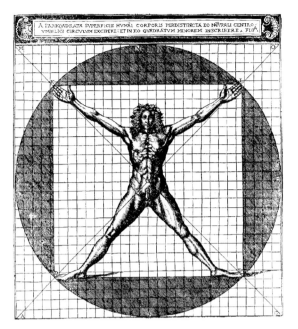

Vitruvian figure from Cesare Cesariano's commentary on Vitruvius, Como 1521

The Roman architectural theorist Vitruvius (c. 84-20 BC) also identified the human body as a model for architecture when describing temples: "No temple can without symmetry and proportion achieve reasonable form unless its elements are in a certain ratio to each other, like limbs of a well-formed human being" (de architectura III/1.1). Number and geometrical form make it possible to apply human dimensions to architecture. Here Vitruvius mentions the circle and the square in particular, into which a human being with outstretched arms and legs can be inscribed (de architectura III/1.3). The "Vitruvian figure" the Middle Ages understood mainly as an abbreviation of the Christian universe acquired central importance in the Renaissance as evidence that had come down from antiquity, which was admired and taken as a model, and related directly to architecture.

These connections were seen not just as expressing metaphysical links, but above all as the rational basis of beauty and a precondition for artistic creativity. The old idea that the human form and mathematical laws correspond to each other also forms the basis of the "Modulor" that Le Corbusier (1887-1965) tried to use to give architecture a mathematical order relating to human scale.

23

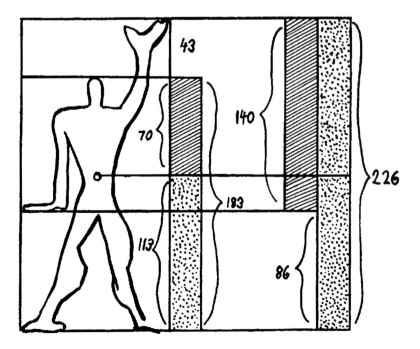

Le Corbusier: The Modulor, 1950

The *correct measure* is one of the most fascinating and at the same time most controversial subjects relating to artistic creativity, oscillating between the poles of freedom and commitment, emotion and reason. Correct measure is a universal principle of classical aesthetics, as a sound relationship between proportions determining the ratio of the parts to each other and to the whole. *Proportion* is a partial aspect of form; it cannot create form, but it regulates emergent form, and lends lasting quality to created form. This applies to architecture in particular. So it is not surprising that crucial sections of architectural theory from Vitruvius to Le Corbusier are proportion theories.

How can architectural proportions be experienced? Architecture's essence and its prime function of satisfying the elemental need for protection and security are to be found in spatial quality. We experience a spatial impression as a three-dimensional phenomenon expansively with our bodies. Here an essential component of the experience is the relationship between the size of our own body and the size of the building, its dimensions. But then we grasp spatial quality pictorially through a geometrical abstraction, by breaking built space down into the surfaces surrounding it. These are accessible above all through their outlines, which we – consciously or unconsciously – relate to assumed verticals and horizontals. Fusing these two basic directions to form areas creates rectangles that are not just mathematically comprehensible as a ratio of height to breadth, but also have an expressive value that can be rising, lying or neutral. This "gestural content" of surface values that can fit together to form a varied interplay of loads and braces, repose and movement, and also appear in linear division as a vertical or horizontal dimensional sequence, goes a long way towards determining the aesthetic impression a building makes. Experiencing, contemplating, judging architecture aesthetically, is thus just as much about weighing and examining gestural content as it is about measuring geometrical forms. Because it is scarcely possible to separate these two components precisely, the process of grasping and judging cannot easily be reversed and used as a key to understanding the design process. The fact is that the creative act, which involves choosing and combining forms and contents to make a form that is logical in its own right, takes place as an inseparable interlocking of intuitive imagination and intellectual control. Here – with a pinch of salt – formal gesture derives from intuition and proportion from intellect. Form, dependent on historical, functional, sociological, stylistic, technical and other limitations, provides the basic character; proportion provides the ordering bond within the gestural composition. Form is bound to time, proportional structure is not. But this certainly does not mean that there is any such thing as ideal proportion as such, nor that a certain way of determining proportion has been applied identically over the centuries at different stylistic periods, as some researchers into proportion aver (and they also each favour a different proportional system as the only possible measure as well). On the contrary, different proportional systems have been used throughout architectural history, and they cannot easily be attached to any particular style.

24

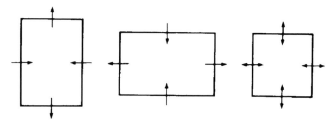

Rectangle "gesture" (after Wolfgang von Wersin)

The fact "that the individual parts create similar figures in form and arrangement" essentially determines the aesthetic quality of a building, according to the similarity theory proposed by the historicist architect August Thiersch (1843-1916). Applied to the temples of antiquity, the proportions of their architectural members (probably developed from building in timber) are seen as a composition made up of rectangular areas – an interpretation confirmed by the results of recent architectural research: according to this, simple, whole-number ratios govern classical temple design not just in terms of their ground plans, but also their elevation. Rational number ratios (1:2, 2:3, 4:9, 5:3, 7:4 etc.) form the abstract basis of Greek temple architecture, deployed in constantly new combinations whose variations essentially confer individuality on a building type that is constant in its typology.

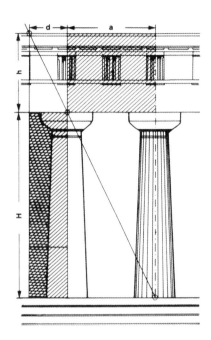

Temple of Poseidon in Paestum (460/450 BC), column placement; proportional scheme (after August Thiersch)

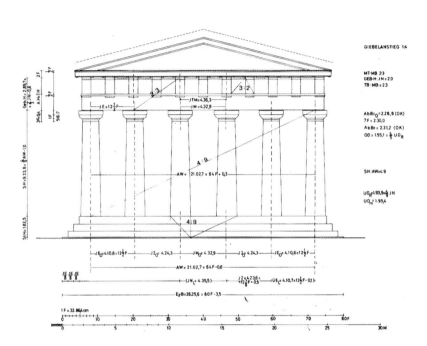

Temple in Segesta (417/409 BC), elevation, proportional scheme (after Dieter Mertens)

The simplest number ratios are among the architectural planning constants we find in almost all phases of architectural history. Two examples – an early medieval ground plan and an elevation from the Baroque period – provide evidence of this. The rational, whole-number proportions of the two buildings can also be seen as corresponding to musical intervals: a note rises in pitch with the number of vibrations in the medium (column of air, gut string etc.) that produces it; conversely it goes down as the medium increases in length. Reflection about the physical fact (allegedly discovered by the Greek philosopher Pythagoras in the 6th century BC) that the vibration ratios of the basic musical intervals correspond to the simplest numerical ratios (octave = 2:1, fifth = 3:2, fourth = 4:3 etc.), led not just to the thought that the harmony of the cosmos is built on these numerical ratios, but also to the idea that these ratios guarantee aesthetic perfection. This Pythagorean/Platonic notion, which was also a constant presence in the Christian Middle Ages, was concretely formulated in architectural terms during the Italian Renaissance by the humanist Leon Battista Alberti (1404-1472). In his extraordinarily influential architectural treatise, written in the mid 15th century, he recommends architects "to derive the whole law of relation from musicians, who know these numbers best" (de re aedificatoria IX/5). Alberti displayed the harmony of musical proportions in his own buildings in a positively virtuoso fashion; but sometimes he also used numbers for his dimensions because of their symbolic significance, here drawing on the spiritual thinking of the Middle Ages: though it is impossible to perceive this visually, the numbers 1, 6, 28 and 496,

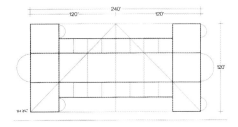

Old cathedral in Cologne (9/10C.), ground plan, proportional scheme (after Arnold Wolff); dimensions in Roman feet at 34.4 cm

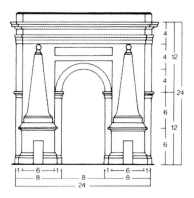

Porte St.-Denis in Paris (François Blondel, 1671-1673), proportional scheme with the architect's modular figures

Palazzo Rucellai in Florence (Leon Battista Alberti, started 1455), façade detail with proportional scheme for the "show areas" framed by pilasters and cornices

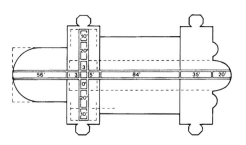

St. Michael's in Hildesheim (started c. 1010), dimensions of the main axes (after Hans Roggenkamp)

26

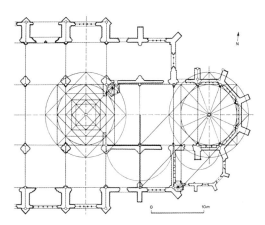

Bern Münster (Matthäus Ensinger, started 1425); ground plan of the eastern half with quadrature drawn in (after Luc Mojon)

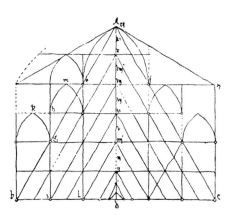

Gabriele Stornaloco: cross section of Milan cathedral; sketch for the report requested by the "Consiglio della Fabbrica" in 1391

for example, known as *numeri perfecti* because of their inherent numerical significance since ancient times (they are identical with the sums of their divisors) determine the axis dimensions of the famous Cluny III abbey church (late 11th century), and the *numeri solidi* 20, 35, 56 and 84 (classified according to ideas of a figurative arrangement of the numbers in surfaces and solids) those of St. Michael's in Hildesheim (early 11th century).

However, "round" numbers are and were used far more frequently in architectural practice, as a rule these are the base numbers of the decimal system (and sometimes the duodecimal system as well), whose preferred status is also reflected by the words for numbers in European languages. And where geometrical figures are used to generate architectural proportions, these almost always start from round-numbered lines, as a rule corresponding with a particularly striking dimension within the building. The coincidence of simple numerical ratios with geometrical figures can be seen most obviously in the square, which is fitted together to form a grid in the ground plan of Old Cologne Cathedral, and determines all the essential lines within the building. But the square's mathematical property of its side being in the ratio of $1:\sqrt{2}$ to the diagonal – an irrational proportion that cannot be expressed in whole numbers – shows a difference in principle between arithmetical and geometrical proportions: the former can be classified mathematically as "commensurable," as "quantities that can be measured by the same measure," while the latter are "incommensurable," as ratios for which there is no common measure" (Euclid, Elements X. def.1). Even though this is not immediately visible in a building, commensurability, which means that the dimensional ratios are comparable (in relation to a fixed unit), corresponds with a very different perception of art from the successive, geometrically constructed emergence of one dimension from another. One of the simplest geometrical proportioning methods – and one of the best documented in the sources – is so-called "quadrature": the central points on a square are connected diagonally, producing a smaller square turned through 45° whose diagonals correspond to the lengths of the sides of the basic square. This process, which can be repeated at will in the opposite direction, produces the sequence of measurements $1:\sqrt{2}:2:2\sqrt{2}:4$ etc. for the sides of the square that follow, i.e. the adjacent measurements in each case are in the irrational ratio of $1:\sqrt{2}$, while the next but one in each case produce the rational ratio 1:2. The crucial feature of this proportioning method, which was used to determine the ratio of length to width of Bern Minster's nave bays, is – regardless of the intersection of rational and irrational dimension ratios – that it is based on successive geometrical construction.

The figure of the triangle is no less fundamental, even though far more complex in terms of form. It is not possible to go into its complex geometry in any more detail here, except to point out the inseparable connection between triangle and circle: different radial divisions of the circle always produce isosceles triangles, which can be understood in their turn as parts of regular polygons (also of squares). Of course the equilateral triangle is the simplest to construct. It is created by plotting the radius on to the circumference of the circle, and in building practice can be created by cutting a piece of cord into three. One of the most important proportions to be detectable in the equilateral triangle, the ratio of the height to the length of the sides, produces the irrational value of $\sqrt{3}:2$. In his famous proportional sketch for the cross-section of Milan cathedral, the mathematician Gabriele Stornaloco established the height of the nave on the basis of an equilateral triangle set up over the width of the nave 96 bracci (=ells), but at the same time expressed the width as the number 84: a rational number that comes as close as possible to the mathematically correct irrational value of the height of the triangle (83, 138 ...). This equilateral triangle is effectively serving as a "divining rod" for establishing the correct ratio of height to width, which was then undoubtedly easier to build using whole-number measurements. So this drawing, one of the very rare medieval sources for the triangle's "defining" function in the architectural planning process, also provides eloquent testimony of ceaseless efforts throughout architectural history to make irrational proportions derived from geometrical operations practicable by using whole-number approximations: thus for example we also find the approximate value 17:12 for the proportion $\sqrt{2}:1$.

A particularly celebrated proportion – and one surrounded by countless speculations – is the so-called "Golden Section." This defines a specific length divided into two unequal sections of which the shorter relates to the longer in the ratio the longer relates to the line as a whole. This "Golden Section," an aesthetic ideal known in ancient times but given its present name only in the 19th century, is classified mathematically as a geometrical series (a:b = b:[a+b]) linked with the comparatively complex geometry of the pentagon that cannot be expressed in rational numbers. So it is not surprising that when used in architecture (as a ratio for lines or areas) its presence can only rarely be reliably proved. Here too the number sequence 1, 1, 2, 3, 5, 8, 13, 21, 34, 55, 89, 144 etc. offers a possibility of approximating to the irrational value of this proportion known in the Renaissance as "divina proportione" in rational numbers: in this sequence, called the "Fibonacci" sequence after the nickname (= filius Bonacci) of the mathematician Leonardo da Pisa (c. 1180-1240), – given the starting sequence 1,1 – each term is the sum of the two preceding terms. Its properties include among others that the quotients of the adjacent terms approximate with increasing precision to the irrational value of the Golden Section. In the model for the dome of the Duomo in Florence (ultimately built differently) the dimensions 55, 89 and 144 bracci are laid down. The two numerical sequences in Le Corbusier's above-mentioned "Modulor" are also Fibonacci sequences in principle, though they do not start with the terms 1, 1, 2, 3 etc. but with figures derived from the average dimensions in centimetres of the human body, 113 or 183 ("red series") and 226 ("blue series"). As Le Corbusier anticipated being able to take figures from both series at random, when the "Modulor" is applied the ratios produced do not only approximate to the Golden Section.

IV

Whichever of the methods – sketched only cursorily and very incompletely here – is used to determine dimensions, the aesthetic impact of a building, whose quality is always based primarily on the imaginative quality of the design, will also depend on the consistency with which a system of proportions is used. This applies conversely to attempts to explain architecture's impact and the processes by which it is created. Results of proportional analysis that cannot be proved from an original source (which is usually the case) can always claim only the status of statements of probability, because "proportion figures" are rarely directly apparent: a representation of a construction process, like for example the one proposed for the Alsatian monastery church in Marmoutier (Maursmünster), gains credibility above all from its mathematical and technical plausibility. The geometrical dimensioning process is easily comprehensible at every stage. And yet no step follows its predecessor as the only possible one inherent in the construction, each is determined by the overriding compositional idea. Some buildings by the American architect Louis I. Kahn (1901-1974) were recently no less convincingly analysed to show that a logical sequence of steps involving figure geometry could also be a factor defining architecture in the 20th century. Of course analyses of this kind require precise structural surveys, the mathematical verifiability of geometrical constructions and a plausible chance of realisation – conditions that are unfortunately not met by the majority of so-called proportional studies, which has brought the genre into general disrepute.

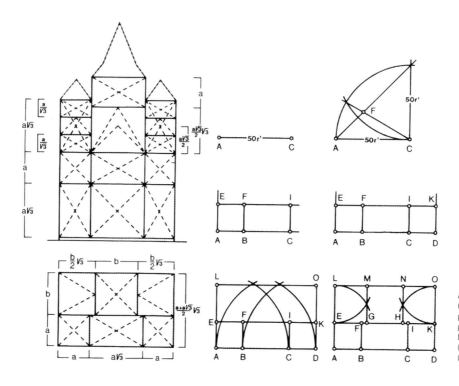

Abbey church in Marmoutier (12C), proportional scheme for ground plan and elevation and geometrical ground plan construction, based on the distance AC (= 50 Roman feet at 29.57 cm) (after Herwig Spieß)

28

The fundamental evaluation of proportions as a factor in artistic creation is no less revealing in terms of understanding creative principles than favouring this or that method of determining proportions. "Ars sine scientia nihil est" declared the French master builder Jean Mignot in the year 1400 at the meeting of the building commission for Milan cathedral, meaning by "scientia" the science of geometry as a basis for establishing proportions. In 1957 a majority of the Royal Institute of British Architects, after an exhaustive discussion, rejected a motion "that systems of proportion make good design easier and bad design more difficult." This vote shows that the conviction late Gothic architects took for granted that freedom and legitimacy are mutually dependent has given way to a scepticism about anything regulated that is typical of our day. But this difference between the two evaluations, lying over half a millennium apart, also reflects the fundamentally ambivalent role played by proportion in architecture: it does not appear directly only as an aesthetic phenomenon, but can also serve as a constructional aid that is not easily discerned: proportion as a phenomenon and/or design scheme.

Literature

Anything even approximating to a full bibliography would be well beyond the scope of this sketch-essay. Hence a few titles are listed here that can be seen as fundamental or exemplary for this subject and/or contain details of other literature. The titles are arranged chronologically in order of the publication year of the first editions.

– August Thiersch: Proportionen in der Architektur, in: Handbuch der Architektur, part 4, half vol. 1,
  3rd ed. Stuttgart 1904 (1st ed. 1883), 37-90
– Theodor Fischer: Zwei Vorträge über Proportionen, 2nd ed. Munich/Berlin 1956 (1st ed. 1934)
– Rudolf Wittkower: Architectural Principles in the Age of Humanism, London 1949
– Le Corbusier: Der Modulor. Darstellung eines in Architektur und Technik allgemein anwendbaren Maßes im Maßstab,
  3rd ed. Stuttgart 1978 (first in French: Le modulor. Essai sur une mesure harmonique, à l'échelle humaine applicable universellement, à l'architecture et à la mécanique, Boulogne/Seine 1950)
– Wolfgang v. Wersin: Das Buch vom Rechteck – Gesetz und Gestik des Räumlichen, Ravensburg 1956
– P. H. Scholfield: The Theory of Proportion in Architecture, Cambridge/Mass. 1958
– Paul v. Naredi-Rainer: Architektur und Harmonie. Zahl, Maß und Proportion in der abendländischen Baukunst,
  7th ed. Cologne 2001 (1st ed. 1982)
– Bauplanung und Bautheorie der Antike. Diskussionen zur archäologischen Bauforschung 4, publ. by the Deutsches Archäologisches Institut, Berlin 1984
– Wolfgang Wiemer: Baugeometrie und Maßordnung der Abteikirche Ebrach – Ergebnisse einer Computeranalyse I. Zugleich Einführung in die Methodik (= Quellen und Forschungen zur Geschichte des Bistums und Hochstifts Würzburg, ed. by Klaus Wittstadt, vol. XLV), Würzburg 1995
– Klaus-Peter Gast: Louis I. Kahn. The Idea of Order, Basel, Berlin, Boston 1998
– Albert van der Schoot: Die Geschichte des Goldenen Schnittes, Stuttgart/Bad Cannstatt 2005 (first in Dutch: De ontstelling van Pythagoras. Over de geschiedenis van de goddelijke proportie, Kampen 1998)
– Richard Padovan: Proportion. Science, Philosophy, Architecture, London/New York 1999

Measurements in Cooking
Renate Breuß

In about 1450, Leon Battista Alberti planned the façade of the Tempio Malatestiano in San Francesco in Rimini with a simple rhythm of open and closed arches. Arches 12 feet wide alternate with piers 6 feet wide in a ratio of 2:1; the height of the springer, set at 18 feet, is in a ratio of 3:2 to the width of the arches. These are simple numerical proportions representing octaves and fifths in the mind of that period, by analogy with the rules of musical intervals. Alberti wanted to offer the eye the same aesthetic pleasure as the equivalent numerical proportions create for the ear.[1]

Leon Battista Alberti: Tempio Malatestiano in San Francesco in Rimini

One of the Renaissance architect Andrea Palladio's principal interests was in creating harmonious proportions not just within a space, but also in the relationship of several spaces to each other.[2] For an unrealised project for a villa in Verona around 1560/70 he designed the ground plan and elevation with simple proportional ratios, using units of 15, 20 and 40 feet. The ground plans of the rooms are in the ratio of 4:3. In order to be able to keep to an even division in three sets of 40 feet for the imposing façade, he reduced the transversely placed front rooms to 36 feet by removing 2 feet from the thickness of the walls in each, thus reducing the octave ratio of 40:20 to a seventh ratio of 36:20.

Designing with tried-and-tested proportional ratios has lost nothing of its validity for the present-day architecture. Bruno Spagolla for example, an important pioneer of the Vorarlberg group of architects which is now acknowledged world-wide, was commissioned to extend and refurbish a primary school, and transferred the proportional ratios of the old building to the new building in his prize-winning design. The hall is 9 m wide, 12 m long and 6 m high – classic three-four time. Starting with basic ratios (4:3, 2:1, 3:2) and orders produced an up-to-date and appropriate solution that gets by without any stylish elements.[3]

[1] cf. Naredi-Rainer, Paul von (1989): Architektur und Harmonie. Zahl, Maß und Proportion in der abendländischen Baukunst. Cologne: DuMont, p. 166

[2] cf. ibid., pp. 177-179

[3] cf. Breuß, Renate (1997): Das Neue als das Rückgrat des Alten. In: Architektur- und Bauforum. Das österreichische Magazin für Baukultur. Vienna: Österreichischer Wirtschaftsverlag

Site plan

Ground floor plan

Bruno Spagolla: primary school in Marul, for which the village won the Sexten international prize in 1997

Cooking as a scientific discipline

Unlike architectural and art history, everyday activities like cooking are hardly ever the subject of scientific research. But an intensive study of historical recipes and the rules inherent in culinary practice makes it possible to identify amazing parallels with artistic creative principles in both cookery and architecture or music. Also, food conveys ideas about changing notions of taste. Unlike buildings and pictures, which remain with us, food is consumed. What does remain is the recipe, and this – rather like the score in music – provides a model that invites interpretation.

Methodically, a recipe can be analysed just as precisely as a picture or a building. In a content-based approach, the objects involved can be identified to begin with. In cooking these can be meat, fish, vegetables or fruit. In painting we recognise a woman, a dog, an angel or a tree, and in the built world a church, a house, a palace or a factory. A description of spices may include an emotional expression about sweet, sour, salty or bitter as flavour qualities, while in pictorial representations we know how to distinguish between a laughing and a weeping angel, and in built form we can separate a powerfully masculine column from a virginally delicate one. The next step is to examine the formal relations as conveyors of meaning, so that an idea of the work in the context of its times can be developed, with knowledge of the prevailing circumstances and historical conditions. In the case of a recipe, it is only then that the actual substance of a food is revealed. Describing the object formally, engaging with the aesthetic structure of a food, shows that this, too, carries meaning and expresses a view of the world. Perceiving a mouthful on the tongue intensively and reading a message from it requires an aesthetic structure and conscious perception. Only then does the food become the sensual proposition of a designed form, does eating admit the gustatory traces of an idea on the tongue.

This essay intends essentially to indicate the scope of rules of measuring and apportioning in cooking, and to make it possible to understand how the forms and proportional ratios used govern flavour and how people can affect their bodies and senses by exploring the world creatively in the field of cooking (or eating).

Man and measure

Until the metric system was introduced in the 19th century man used his own body as a model for recipe measurement units. This can be seen on several levels: in the names of foods, in the quantities used, in shapes and sizes, in the way things are perceived by the tongue and palate.

In a similar way to anthropomorphic architectural concepts, like for example Francesco Giorgio Martini's church ground plan of 1480/1490 relating to human dimensions, parts of a food are also compared to human limbs and organs. In church architecture we have the head of the choir, the transept arms and the body of the building itself, and in the language of cookery we have plaited loaves, garlic heads, salad hearts, ladies' fingers and *orecchiette*, liver and kidneys, tongue and pork belly. These names derive from the existing similarity to the part of the human body or its influence on the shape created, as in a loaf that is plaited like hair. In the Bregenzerwald (Vorarlberg, Austria), there used to be a cake called *Ault wibar knüe* (old woman's knee). "It was made by dipping a dried damson or similar into the dough and baking it; this little cake was then dipped into the dough again and baked once more. If this process is repeated two to three times, large knobbly shapes emerge that are then coarsely compared with old women's knees."[4]

[4] quoted from Breuß, Renate (1999): Das Maß im Kochen. Mengen und Maßangaben in Kochrezepten von der Antike bis zur Einführung der metrischen Maße im 19. Jahrhundert und deren Parallelität zu künstlerischen Gestaltungsprinzipien, Innsbruck: Haymon, p. 56

Today analogies with parts of our own bodies are avoided wherever possible when naming food. It once seemed quite natural that human beings are close to the material of food, but this has since become taboo. We no longer see qualitative comparisons like "let the quinces cook so that they can still be grasped" or "sugar the almond milk to be as sweet as cow's milk." What is happening much more is that current food presentation is being aestheticised. The senses and sensuality are mentioned, but the image of the closeness of the manufacturing process to the material, to the body, has slipped somewhat out of focus. This physicality, sensually oriented towards the material, sometimes between the lines as well, is still present in old cookery books.

The quantities used in cooking provide a parallel with the direct transfer of the human form to architectural designs. Originally there was a very direct, simple connection. Starting with the individual human being with "his appetite" and "his hunger," then the correct quantity for daily nutritional needs was via "his handful." These fluctuating quantities, based on a well developed man of normal size, became fixed when measures were standardised in a generalised system. The Greek measure *choenix* for dry goods and corn applied the normal quantity for a daily ration, calculated for a grown man, to a fixed system of measures. The German volume unit for dry goods was the *Metzen*, which goes back to a grain ration the size of a fist. It remains established culinary practice to take a handful of basic ingredients like flour, noodles or rice per person and use this quantity as a basic measure or module. If hearty or small eaters are expected at the table, an extra handful, a man's handful or a little handful are added. When pieces are being served, the rank and hierarchy of the eaters is taken into account. So quantity can be conveyed in a qualitative formulation, and conversely a sense of quantity can be established via purely perceptive descriptions. Sight is not lost of the undivided whole, which as well as the number of people can also be the vessel, the foodstuff, the whole fish. Other orders and divisions can be derived from this.

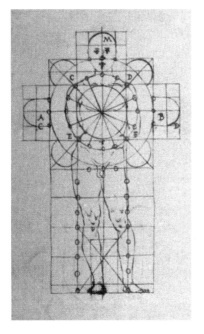

Francesco Giorgio Martini: church ground plan dating from 1480/1490

In addition to their limbs people also influence culinary creativity via their senses and body language. So the finishing touches are put to food by using all the senses: how does the dough feel, what does a chop look like in the frying-pan, what can I hear, what can I smell? The cook can hear and see the end of a cooking time from the sizzling sound or the colour *laz es also lange braten biz daz es singe und rot werde* ("let it fry till that it shall sing and redden"). He can smell from the fragrance rising whether enough herbs have been added, he structures a dough by stirring, kneading and working, gesturally and rhythmically, he establishes the right consistency for dumplings with his hand and fingers, assesses quantities and areas, measures spatial ratios. Technical measuring devices are more precise as such, but man and his senses are more accurate in finding the right connection, in bringing together (composing), in tasting as the final authority.

Cooks insisted on constant tasting of food in their early writings: until it's right. "The cook who relies on his own sense of taste will never be a bad cook. You will never go wrong if your sensual organs are clear and in order. Cook and taste often! Not enough salt: add some more. Something else missing: try it, taste it until it's right, until the taste is correct; pluck like a harp until it is in tune. And when you think everything is in tune, then produce your chorus of foods in singing harmony."[5]

[5] Machon quoted from Breuß, 1999, p. 39f

Matching, paying attention, being right

Pre-metric recipes constantly allude to adapting, paying attention and being right. "And the said master should pay attention that he does not add too much of anything, but has a moderate and controlled hand, and only adds what he thinks fit."[6]

[6] Chiquart quoted from ibid., p. 83

For the Greeks, harmony meant matching parts to the whole. In boat-building this could be fitting two tree trunks together to make a raft or in cooking combining flour and butter to create a new and fitting whole, a crumb-like dough. Viewing harmony as uniting opposites goes back to the mythological figure of Harmonia, who appears in Hesiod (700 BC) as the daughter of the war-god Ares and Aphrodite, the goddess of beauty and love. The concept of harmony was stated mathematically by the Pythagoreans, who discovered the mutual correspondence of notes and numbers, of qualities and quantities in their number theory. If the ratio on a string starting to vibrate on a monochord is 1:2, you hear an octave; if it is 2:3, you hear a fifth, and in a ratio of 3:4 a fourth. The fact that an octave expresses half a whole – whether it is on the string of a musical instrument, a drawn line or a lump of butter – was once seen as general knowledge and also affected culinary practice. "It's starting to look like art, isn't it?," says a cook in a play by Damoxenus (3rd century BC). And then: "As you see I'm mixing according to higher harmony: some things have something in common according to the fourth, others relate to the fifth or the octave. I combine everything according to its own intervals, and weave this together to create a series of appropriate courses. Sometimes I supervise it all with reprimands like: 'Why are you adding that?,' 'What do you want to mix in here?,' 'Watch out, you're plucking a dissonant string.'"[7] Consonant sounds are preferred, i.e. proportions consisting of low whole numbers. The fact that a quantity can change into quality, and this is seen as a value, is also expressed by the much-quoted "correct measure," keeping to the happy or correct medium. In 1485, in the oldest printed German cookery book, the master cook demands: *Ob du dy mos recht kanst treffen so bistu ein guter koch* ("If you can meet the right measure you are a good cook"). In Albrecht Dürer's words: "There is a correct medium between too much and too little; you must try to meet this in all your works." He wanted to know "what would be the right measure and no other." Dürer used the word "measure" (*mas*) as a term synonymous with proportion, and understood it to mean "the harmony of the whole coming together of the whole ensemble."[8] Here quantitative as well as qualitative aspects are to be considered, masculine should not be mixed with feminine, fat figures with thin ones, youth not mixed with age.

[7] Athenaeus quoted from ibid., p.132f

[8] quoted from ibid., p.72

As in painting and architecture, choosing the correct proportions is also part of the form giving process in cooking. Proportion regulates the ratio obtaining between several parts. Just as for the medieval master builder the rules of proportion contain basic static formulae, the practical value of any rule that is used in the kitchen is a precondition, i.e. a dough may not crumble, it must hold together statically, and at the same time satisfy dietary ideas, as well as ideas of flavour. Culinary formulations about ratios and proportions are simple. So we say "take twice as much of one than the other; for *Kässpätzle* (a kind of cheese noodle) take three parts mountain cheese, two parts Räss cheese and one part Emmentaler." Hildegard von Bingen would have said: "take Emmentaler, twice as much Räss cheese and as much mountain cheese as both together." The personal, the individual quality is expressed here by slight deviations from an ideal type (9:8) – a little more, a soupçon less. Dividing into halves, thirds or quarters can usually be done by eye. What is important is to work to proportions fundamentally, the appropriate relation of the parts to a whole, and to the demands of quality. The simple intelligibility of these ratios has however tended to be forgotten when converting to metric equivalents. There, one part butter and two parts flour can be more readily achieved visually that by the precise weights 280g and 560g.

Good rice

[9] for this see Naredi-Rainer (1989) in the "Proportionen" chapter, p. 186 ff

The Golden Section shows that man used his own body as a model for proportions that were seen as balanced. People assumed their innate measuring tools like ell, foot, hand and finger were equal to the Golden Section proportions in their subdivisions. But in fact they relate to the ratios of the Fibonacci series,[9] a sequence of numbers that is similar to the Golden Section in its successive division. In cooking, the ratio of 5:8 is found in surface and in volume measures: If I draw a rectangle around my "well-formed finger," it comes out about 5 cm wide and 8 cm high. It is normal practice in recipes to cut something "two

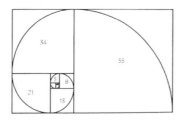

Golden section and Fibonacci series

fingers wide and one finger long." In a Sicilian Caponata, a vegetable dish, the key ingredients are in a ratio of 5:8 to each other. The cook from the Benedictine monastery of *Sant'Andrea Apostolo alle Vergini* in Palermo put it like this at the end of the last century: "It is difficult to give exact quantities for foods of this kind. All you can do is bear in mind that the aubergines and the courgettes make the dish, and all the other ingredients are seasonings (capers, olives, vinegar, sugar), and that 800g of aubergines and 1/2kg of courgettes will be enough for six people."[10] In good Chinese kitchens the ratio of rice to water is 1:1.6, i.e. five parts of rice are boiled in eight parts of water. The Austrian cook Zenker gave the following description of beating egg-whites: "180 strokes in the first minute, 200 in the second, 230 in the third, 280 in the fourth and 360 strokes in the fifth minute." The increasing number of strokes from the first to the fifth minute is like a Fibonacci sequence: 20, 30, 50, 80. Similar efforts were made in music at the same time, fixing the length of a note precisely by counting. The metronome was patented to measure musical time by Johann Nepomuk Mälzel in 1816, Zenker wrote his recipe down in 1817/18.

So the simplest numerical ratios do not just form the design basis for Greek temples, Palladio's villas and the school at Marul. The ratios in which dough, soups and sauces are mixed contain the most frequently used ratios of octave, fifth and fourth, encompassing the numbers 1, 2, 3 and 4. According to the Italian architect and theoretician Leon Battista Alberti, these are

[10] quoted from ibid., p.78

[11] quoted from Museum für Gestaltung (ed.) (1991): Die gute Form. Teigwaren aller Art. Basel: Schwabe & Co AG, p. 18

musical numbers. "He was convinced that buildings containing these numerical proportions give the eyes as much aesthetic pleasure as the notes corresponding with them do for the ear." Aesthetic delight for the tongue is the continuation for this quotation that springs to mind. The philosopher Lichtenberg surmised that the tongue might assess surfaces or solids in the same way the ear measures ratios.[11]

Reading form on the tongue

[12] Rumohr, Karl Friedrich von (1922): Geist der Kochkunst. Munich: Georg Müller. p. 79 (first edition Stuttgart, Tübingen 1822)

[13] quoted from Breuß, 1999, p. 116

The great number of descriptions of form in recipes suggests that the relationships between form and taste were known everywhere. The art historian Karl Friedrich von Rumohr was not alone in describing, in the *Geist der Kochkunst* in 1822, the formal play with contrasts, and how they affect taste: "The sweetness and mildness of the eel acquires a very agreeable contrast in the crust for which I have just given instructions."[12] In a baroque recipe for scrambled almond pancakes, a pound of almonds is first of all divided into three parts: "chop the first part coarsely, the second cut lengthways, and leave the third part whole..." To make a pâté from the comb, liver and testicles of a cock: "Cut each comb into three parts and the liver into four parts, and leave the testicles whole." Comparative sizes also give an insight into a cook's personal and cultural environment. In monastery kitchens, *Schaumgebäck* (lit. "foam cake") was "as large as hosts," and the painting on the chocolate biscuits copied "the kings and queens in packs of cards." The Austrian cook Zenker larded the whole goose liver with truffles, "...to which end the same were cut into the shape of those nails that are to be seen in the holy paintings, e.g. on the holy cross, where only the heads stick out; ..."[13]

Personal qualities like generosity and miserliness, as well as aesthetic criteria, can be expressed through form, whether foods are diced, shredded, cut into strips or discs or left whole. If you want to save meat, or don't have very much of it, you simply cut it smaller. We are all aware that potatoes boiled in their skins taste different with butter and salt from the same potatoes if mashed. We all have our preferences, whether it is for wafer-thin chocolate or thick ribs, whole nuts or nut slivers, thickly or thinly sliced bread. Our tongues are very well able to detect the most subtle differences, even if we cannot define them precisely.

Verbal description is not enough to build up a flavour experience and train our imaginations. This can only be done by tasting: if you offer two shortbread biscuits to taste, one in the ratio of 2:1 and one in the ratio of 3:2, i.e. one economical, one fine, it is soon clear: both are good, and the more economical version can certainly hold its own with the finer one. It is just a question of proportions. Mies van der Rohe called it "less is more."

The following list shows how proportional ratios are used in the same way
in cooking, music and architecture

Unison   1:1   as much of one as of the other

1 part flour, 1 part butter (short pastry, genoise mixture, royal pie dough)

other examples: roux, marzipan, marinade, equal weight cake

Architecture: the Holy of Holies in the Temple at Jerusalem

Great whole tone   9:8   9 parts butter, 8 parts flour (good butter dough)

Expressing a very slight deviation from unison, give a preference to butter

In culinary language: take the same amount of butter as flour, give a preference to butter

Architecture: Alberti, Palazzo Rucellai, façade: the central axis is a whole tone

wider than the other axes

Fourth   4:3   4 parts almonds, 3 parts sugar (marzipan, more economical variant)

Expressing a greater deviation, for example at times when sugar is in short supply,

but the ratio still works

Architecture: Spagolla, Marul primary school

Fifth   3:2   3 parts flour, 2 parts butter (fine short pastry)

Architecture: Francesco di Giorgio Martini, church ground plan

following the dimensions of a human being

Minor sixth   8:5   8 parts water, 5 parts rice (Chinese rice)

Architecture: Le Corbusier, Modulor with Fibonacci series

Major sixth   5:3   5 parts flour, 3 parts butter (fine pie dough)

Architecture: Alberti, Palazzo Rucellai, façade, show areas

Minor seventh   9:5   A little less than double as much of one as the other

Architecture: Alberti, Palazzo Rucellai, façade, show areas

Major seventh   15:8   only a tiny bit less than double as much of one as of the other

Architecture: Alberti, Palazzo Rucellai, façade, show areas

Octave   2:1   twice as much of one as of the other

2 parts flour, one part butter (more economical short pastry)

Architecture: Bramante, Tempietto, San Pietro in Montorio

Karl Krimes: from a dining room, 1919

Materials and Colours
Annette Gigon in Conversation with Petra Hagen Hodgson

P.H.H.: Seen in terms of the history of civilisation, building and cooking are existential human activities. Do you feel that building houses and preparing food are still related to satisfying basic needs?

A.G.: There are indeed some parallels between constructing buildings and preparing food. As you say, this is partly because we human beings cannot manage without the products of these two activities. But the same also applies to making clothing. Clothes and buildings are even more essentially related. Architecture can definitely been seen as stiff coverings; coverings that – except in fairytales – may not be made of edible components. But buildings are different from clothes in that they are much bigger and heavier, cover and occupy land, create places. Architecture changes the surface of the earth, architecture is material processed and transformed to make the surface of the earth bigger, to make it contain space. It is of course also possible to say of food growing, the step that proceeds food preparation, that it changes the face of the earth – affecting it less deeply, but over a greater area.

P.H.H.: Rules and recipes for the way ingredients are put together that have come down over the centuries form the basis of cooking. Building, too, follows conventions and rules, works with ratios of proportion and scale. Both building and cooking aim to satisfy demands relating to aesthetics or taste. Your buildings have a harmony of their own. They are well balanced. Do your buildings emerge from playing with the rules of architecture alone, or do you take account of changing perceptual demands as well?

A.G.: Let me digress about that briefly: for an exhibition in the architectural gallery in Lucerne in 1993 we put out specimens of all the materials that made up our first buildings, or that we had assessed for those buildings. We compared this display with a *mise en place* – a term from gastronomy (and show kitchens) for the prepared ingredients ready to be made into a dish. We did this partly to draw attention to how important materials are to us, but we were also interested in "dissecting" the buildings into their components, and finally we liked the construction kit aspect. Materials that seemed ugly because they were used in industrial building were included, or some that were barely recognisable because they aren't usually left visible. Materials that you could "wake up" by using them differently. In the context of your question about scale and proportion, it is interesting that the dimensions and proportions of a body or a room are not absolutely right or wrong, but that they are better or worse according to the materials they are executed in. A wooden room looks quite different from a stone room of exactly the same size.

Werkstoff ("working materials") exhibition at the architecture gallery Lucerne 1993. The exhibits were aids like material specimens used in architectural planning

We use models of different scales to determine dimensions and proportions – by eye much more than by using the rules of proportion. But in architecture this search has to happen within the boundaries of those rules and regulations called function, construction, budget and building laws. The last-named are usually the decisive "measures."

P.H.H.: The materials used or the ingredients and the specific way they are treated are important for both creative activities, cooking and building. Your projects excel because material and construction contribute considerably to perfecting expression. Do these projects arise from reducing and refining the ingredients or from reinventing and differentiating them?

A.G.: Both things are true. The former is more the case for the Kirchner Museum. There we took a familiar material, glass, and treated it differently and used it differently according to the role the glass had to play in relation to handling the light and transparency when looking into the museum interior. We used clear, etched and also profiled glass. And then we spread broken glass, i.e. waste glass on the flat roofs instead of gravel. But for the Oskar Reinhart Collection on the Römerholz in Winterthur it was the latter, the invention of a new concrete mixture. We were trying to match the new part of the building to the existing historic villa (1915) and its gallery extension (1924) in terms of material rather than form and detail. We wanted a concrete façade and at the same time a patina that formed quickly, as occurs with metals, particularly copper. So we started by adding finely powdered copper to the concrete. But we didn't get the change to green colouring we were looking for until we used a concrete mixture that also had limestone added. Incidentally, both the copper and the limestone were materials used for the existing villa. The unusual concrete mixture can also be seen as a kind of alchemistic approximation to this difficult *genius loci*.

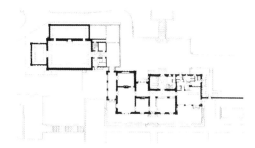

Ground plan

Oskar Reinhart collection "Am Römerholz," Winterthur, 1993/1995-1998

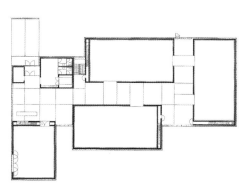

Ground plan

Kirchner Museum Davos, 1989-1992

P.H.H.: Cooking always has regional connections. Your buildings always relate to their location. How do you "cook" this relation? How do you tackle tradition and a sense of belonging, without slipping into regionalisms?

A.G.: The location is very important in our work. We can relate to it on a large number of levels. Sometimes it is impossible to avoid connecting up with the local building tradition because it is imposed to a certain extent by building legislation, as for example in the case of the gallery store in Wichtrach, a small rural town in the canton of Bern. Here the local regulations for protecting the townscape insist on pitched roofs protruding by at least a metre for new buildings. We met these conditions, suspended a transparent façade layer from the roof protrusions as a climatisation curtain, but clad the building in the material that is not just used locally but globally for storage facilities – tetra sheets. But frequently we try to pin down local connections ourselves, to "locate" the building. The Museum Liner is an example of this. There we tried to respond to the intricacy of the landscape by creating a strongly articulated structure made up of an accumulation of individual buildings or spaces. The sheet chromium steel façade cladding serves to reflect the neutrally coloured diffuse light from the shed roofs. Even though they were considerably bigger, and show different material qualities, the overlapping sheets are reminiscent of the traditional way of building with little wooden shingles. The most unusual but in effect the most direct local link is to be found in the archaeological museum and park in Bramsche-Kalkriese near Osnabrück. There the location is not just the site and the context, but the actual reason why the building is there. It is the place where two thousand years ago the Germanic tribes fought their famous battle against the Romans, known as Varus's battle, or the *Hermannsschlacht* or (wrongly) the Battle of the Teutoburger Wald. All the architectural interventions we introduced are in steel, in the form of structural steel, Larsen sections, tubular steel, sheet steel for the façade cladding and to cover the footpaths; steel processed in different ways and in different alloys; painted, oiled, galvanised, rusting. Steel in these dimensions has been available only since industrialisation, and thus dates the contemporary intervention. But even so it alludes to the intricate metal objects, the coins, shoe nails, lead shot for slings and face masks that have been excavated from the Roman period. Finally, the various conditions the steel materials are in convey the aspect of the temporal, the transitory.

Art-Depot gallery Henze & Ketterer, Wichtrach near Bern, 2002-2004

Archaeological Museum and Park in Bramsche-Kalkriese, 1998-2002

Museum Liner, Appenzell, 1996-1998

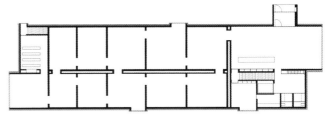

Ground plan

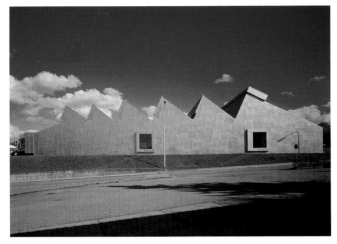

Museum Liner, Appenzell

Museum Liner, Appenzell

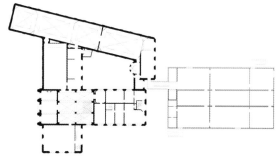

Ground plan

Extension of the art museum Winterthur, 1993-1995

P.H.H.: "Everything good," the French writer Curnonsky once said, "tastes of what it is." Here he is raising the issue of ingredients, their quality as materials and their natural taste. Architectural Modernism introduced the moral categories of "honesty"and "doing justice to materials" in order to insist on high-quality materials. Are these still criteria that you address? I feel that you are now concerned about something more, about something different: about effects and moods, about physical, visual experiences, about pure material beauty.

A.G.: In the half-canton of Appenzell Innerrhoden the buildings are absolutely beautiful, painted in bright colours, while in the half-canton of Appenzell Ausserrhoden, where I grew up, the traditional buildings are white or wood-coloured. We have these two poles in our work as well. On the one hand there are the buildings that make their effect simply through construction and material, like the Kirchner Museum we've already mentioned, or the museum extension in Winterthur. Both of these take the concept of honesty even further in that they also allow some insight into the way the façade is constructed. Then there are the buildings whose appearance we have tried to enhance with colour. Colour is a very reasonably priced and also an enormously powerful tool here. It changes, covers or conceals building material. Perhaps colour really could be compared with spices, where you need only a very little to change the taste of food. For the Broëlberg I residential complex, one of our first coloured buildings, we even tried to use colour as a cognitive element. We coloured a rendered, external insulation façade dark brown and bright orange. We wanted to use the colours, which are unusual for rendering, alienating and reminiscent of organic things, to indicate what was under them, which was not mineral masonry of concrete, but (chemically) organic insulation material. We do actually try to make our buildings calm, relaxed, striking, charismatic, and also beautiful – regardless of whether we use colour or not. But something that is just as important for us is the convincing quality, the coherence of a project, the way the parts relate to each other. Do they follow an inner logic, or are they simply an accumulation of interesting details.

Residential housing Broelberg I, Kilchberg, 1994-1996

Ground plan

P.H.H.: When preparing food there is a close link between colour and the appetite stimulated by it. And in architecture as well there is a close interplay between colour and whether viewers will "involve themselves." Your colours do not just convey moods, but above all define parts of buildings and spaces. You work with artists in order to achieve this. Can you explain the importance of colour in building? In this context, I am also interested in how your involvement with art has influenced your work. You have built several art museums and worked directly with artists on a number of occasions.

A.G.: We have used colour for a whole variety of reasons, and also in very different ways, according to the concept behind the building. We usually brought in artists who can pilot us through the "colour cosmos:" Adrian Schiess, Harald F. Müller, Pierre André Ferrand. Again I can best explain our different approaches by using examples. For the little signal box in Zurich we noticed the brownish-red stains on the buildings and objects near the tracks caused by the fine iron dust released when the trains apply their brakes, and this suggested adding iron oxide pigments to our concrete. For the Susenbergstrasse residential development on the Zürichberg we allotted different colours to the three buildings to make them more individual and thus relate them to the surrounding villas. Here, the colour is applied in the form of mineral pigments. For the Pflegi site residential development in Zurich the colour was restricted to three areas, to colour the outside spaces, to "flavour" them, while the rest of the façade surfaces were left in their natural concrete colour. Perhaps I should add that when working with artists neither we nor they were interested in making architecture into works of art you can walk into. What we were trying to do in these buildings, and what the artists gave us in their different ways, was that they should contribute to our architecture in a way that fitted in with their character and their artistic interests. They contributed in the spirit of thinking together, searching together, looking together and creating the architecture together. The artistic work is so strongly built into the design concept of the buildings that the elements of art and architecture can scarcely be separated. This contrasts with the familiar "art in building" situation, but also with the museum buildings, where there is a clear distinction between the buildings and the art on show there. We did not use colour for most of our museum buildings, leaving the colour to the art, so to speak. But for the sake of completeness I must mention the exceptions – the Römerholz Collection with its self-pigmented patina and the museum Albers Honegger *Espace de l'art concrète* in Mouans-Sartoux, France, which stands in the middle of a little château park. The tower-like building is painted in a yellowish-green mineral colour which harmonises or contrasts with the surrounding trees according to the season, but it is also a colour anticipating the discoloration that algae and moss will cause later.

44

Three residential houses at the Susenbergstraße, Zurich, 1998-2000

Pre-station signal box, Zurich, 1996-1999

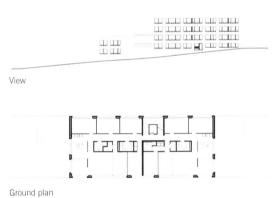

View

Ground plan

Residential housing Pflegi-Areal, Zurich, 1998-2002

Residential housing Pflegi-Areal, Zurich

Residential housing Pflegi-Areal, Zurich

P.H.H.: Over and above mere usefulness, both architecture and cooking are referred to as art: the art of building *(Baukunst)* and the art of cooking *(Kochkunst)*. Both convey values and ideas. Annette Gigon, your works are moving, create spaces that relate to each other sensually. What guiding design thoughts lead to your buildings acheiving this quality?

A.G.: They are probably not so much thoughts as visions, concepts, ideas that drive the design work. And besides the actual work of producing plans it is above all the working with models that makes it possible to check and correct our ideas – and we also use trial and error, by trying to generate new solutions by adapting the model. To an extent this trying out is comparable with tasting when cooking, checking the flavours. I am not particularly fond of the term *Baukunst* (literally "the art of building") even though it does suggest the idea that this intensive, patient, sometimes desperate search for convincing solutions produces a kind of added value corresponding with the utility value. But it is not the case that this *Baukunst* label will bring about a shift in discipline to fine art. Even though there are a large number of shared approaches, great mutual interest and various ways of working together, there is still a crucial difference between fine art and architecture (and cooking): fine art does not have a function to fulfil, a purpose to serve, it defines itself, chooses its own subjects and resources – at least since the 20th century. Fine artists might cook like Rirkrit Tiravanija, offer food on a naked woman as Meret Oppenheim once did, make furniture like Franz West and Joep van Lieshout or Jorge Pardo. They do this within the perimeter that art has extended for itself – still always complying with mimesis, artistic training and replicating the world. And this does not make them cookery or design artists.

P.H.H.: Food speaks to all our senses. We taste and smell above all through our noses. How important is the sensory perception of architecture to you? Should buildings smell? Could they be even perceived acoustically and via their tactile qualities?

A.G.: People very rarely touch buildings. Its true we stand in them, and walk about, but only a very few elements are intended to be touched – looked at conversely, it is the things in a building that "take us by the hand" to a certain extent, let us in, take us through the rooms, make us able to "handle" it: doorknobs and window fastenings, handrails, fittings and electric switches. Another factor affecting the way a building opens up to us is the way footsteps and voices echo. There are rooms in the canton of the Grisons that smell, even smell good, and go on doing so for decades because they are clad in Swiss stone pine. This is an attractive exception, otherwise I am pleased if rooms do not smell of anything, do not have hard acoustics and are light, so that you can breathe in them, work, talk, dream, eat and drink in them.

P.H.H.: Finally: we know you as a good architect. Do you cook too? Do you prefer any particular cuisine? If so, why?

A.G.: I like raw things very much: fruit, salads, vegetables. This is probably what holds me back – as well as a very busy diary – from extending my little repertoire of dishes. I do like cooking, spaghetti with tomatoes and garlic, for example, fish with ginger and leeks, sauerkraut with apples, onions and bacon – in other words not just Swiss cooking. But we quite often have a meal of fresh ravioli from a little shop in our neighbourhood.

48

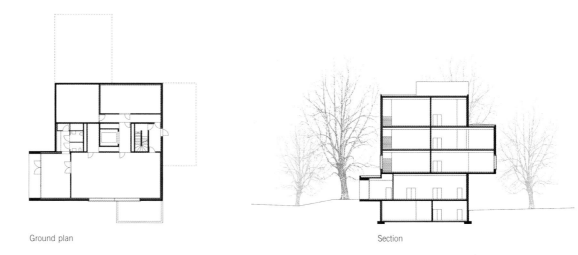

Ground plan   Section

Espace de l'art concrete, Mouans-Sartoux, France, 1999-2003

The Homely Hearth
Building and Living, Eating and Drinking, Considered in Terms of Architectural Theory
Fritz Neumeyer

"There's no place like home." Popular saying

I

[1] Walzel, Oskar: Wechselseitige Erhellung der Künste, Berlin 1917

Regarding the skilfull combination of raw materials to "useful" and "beautiful" ends, there is a deeply rooted cultural-historical relationship between the arts of cooking and construction. The interplay and parallels between these two practical arts have not yet found their way into standard considerations of *Wechselseitige Erhellung der Künste* ("mutual illumination by the arts") – the title of a study by Oskar Walzel,[1] comparing architecture and music, among other things. But there are a number of linking factors that suggest themselves on closer examination, and justify detailed treatment.

The art of building and the art of cooking are definitely close to each other as basic, practical activities; both are concerned with the existential production of the means to live: food, which sustains and nourishes the body, and built work to give permanent, sheltering accommodation. Preparing easily digestible solid food and constructing stable shelter are among the anthropological constants of human culture. It is no coincidence that the German language includes viticulture (*Weinbau*) and agriculture (*Ackerbau*) within the higher conceptual field of construction activities (*Bau-Wesen*), so the latter one is by no means the exclusive domain of architecture. Language is also part of this basic culture production, with its sentence construction (*Satzbau*). The significance for human life of the "art of construction", or architecture, is taken for granted and yet profound and complex, as is revealed in the cultural sphere by "eating and drinking", which cannot be imagined without agriculture and viticulture. As far as consuming and preparing food and drink is concerned, probably every one has direct, comprehensive experience here. Everyone has been involved in cooking in some way in the course of their lives, even if it is only cooking an egg for breakfast. There is a much more marked division of labour in construction, however. Despite the popularity of do-it-yourself stores and a widespread mentality to match, the role of the consumer seldom corresponds to that of the producer.

I was compelled to see that there is a connection worth investigating between architecture and cooking by my own culinary and artistic taste experiences and preferences. Here travel made a lasting impression, and Italy comes first as a country inviting travel – how could it be otherwise. Nowhere else have I seen so many beautiful buildings and cities, and so revelled in art and architecture, nowhere else have I feasted with such delight and in such abundance and tasted such staggeringly sumptuous wines, the latter above all in Piedmont. It was in Italy I acquired a taste for tasting. Here standards that made a lasting impact on my taste-memory were set for physical and sensual delights and for architecture (and also for some other beautiful things that are not relevant here). It must be possible to take home a powerful sense that there must be mysterious bonds between architecture and the culture of cooking and eating that go beyond coincidence, forming a living cultural entity, from any country in which cooking and eating mean a way of life.

As we all know, eating is not just about the food itself, which must be nourishing, tasty and appetising, but above all about the ambience as well, the whole performance that goes on round about it. And architecture is one of the elements supplying a not unimportant part of this context, in which "eating" features as a complex cultural and social "event." Cooking and eating culture always take place in an architectural setting, as preparing and consuming food usually needs a more or less solid spatial framework. This is offered by the domesticity of our own or someone else's four walls, or beyond the private sphere, an appropriate place in a public area.

Even when we talk about eating in the open air we are fundamentally thinking of a place that is contained spatially, and may be architecturally designed. Even a picnic will at least have a blanket spread out, so that a table can be laid on the ground as well. Our preferred places for eating in the open air are terraces, something half-open like a pergola or loggia, whose spatial world in a particularly privileged position sometimes means that it is also possible to include nature in the picture, as a landscape showpiece. Courtyards and gardens are also popular places to eat, and pleasant to linger in. But of course busy places

51

like the pavement in a street or ultimately an urban square are immensely popular places to eat. The old European urban quality that makes it possible to sit in the open air as if in a great banqueting hall is obviously still one of the preferred places as far as our eating habits are concerned. But consuming food and also drink is not necessarily the main issue. Enjoying the public quality itself is a factor in its own right, and the position in which we are placed in the space is sometimes more important than the act of consumption, which is just a reason, the admission ticket, as it were, for being able to sit at a table and delight in ancient urban drama of seeing and being seen, which constantly stages new versions of itself. What would this "performance" be without a fixed architectural or urban framework? Just as the theatre finds its architectural form in the playhouse with its stalls, circles and boxes, an open-air show also needs its architectural framework.

Eating culture is linked with the rituals of a world of experience in which the joy of being alive is transformed into art. Enhancing and celebrating life are essential elements in the meaning and purpose of art. The art of life lies above all in making the everyday into something special, namely an "event." Art is, according to a saying of Nietzsche, the highest affirmation of existence in enhancing the sense of life through the beautiful. In the case of cooking, which like architecture links the necessary and the beautiful with each other, the life-enhancing function of the art is immediately clear. As has already been suggested, architecture and cooking both belong under the heading of the "art of necessity," to borrow

Italian dining culture: Massa Marittima

a concept that the philosopher F.W.J. Schelling once applied to architecture. So the real joy of eating occurs when what is necessary for nourishment is indivisibly linked with beauty of flavour. And like every real joy, the joy of eating, as something that satisfies physical necessity and as delight in the sensually beautiful, enhances our physical and mental well-being and thus shifts us into a notably more pleasant mood, which we can probably all adequately confirm from our own experience.

So transforming eating into an uplifting "experience" or a work of art means nothing less than transforming the necessary intake of nourishment into a sensual feast for eye, nose and palate, and thus heightening it. If this is successful, then the present state of things makes us naturally, strangely and expectantly excited, which brings our whole nervous machine up to speed. At this moment the natural unity of the creating and the consuming individual re-emerges. Enjoyable consumption makes us communicative, we want to tell the person next to us at table about ourselves, we come out of ourselves. Our attitude, expressions and gestures become expressive, enthusiasm makes our voices take on onomatopoeic tonal inflections when the food and drink taste excellent, language looks for colourful words, rich images to describe superlative experiences, in brief, in the pleasurable, elated enjoyment of art we seem to become a little poetic and artistic ourselves. Hölderlin's beautiful phrase *Dichterisch wohnet der Mensch auf dieser Erde* ("Poetically dwells mankind upon this earth") could also be interpreted in culinary terms on the basis of this voluptuous, enhanced form of existence.

18ᵗʰ century fireplace, Isola on the Splügen pass

Cooking and architecture are primarily linked by the social aspect. Architecture is an art that creates society, making certain forms of community possible; eating culture claims and demands community: there is nothing more desolate and uncultivated than filling your belly on your own. Preparing and consuming food communally is one of the most appropriate ways of promoting a sense of community. The "urban quality" of eating, as it were, is to be found in this state of affairs. This is also the reason for the quasi-religious significance of a shared meal like the "Last Supper." Communication enhances enjoyment and is what really makes eating into an experience, because sensuality and sociability come into their own to an equal extent through coming together at table.

Creating social experience of this kind begins in a domestic framework and on the smallest architectural scale with laying the table, arranging various little vessels like glasses, bowls and plates used to store and present food and drink appropriately. The morphology of the vessels continues into the next spatial dimension via table, chair and wall, to the architectural spatial vessel known as the "dining room." It can also go beyond the private and interior spheres and end up in a large collective spatial vessel, in an open-air "dining room," perhaps in an urban square full of restaurants and laid tables, looking irresistibly inviting.

52

II

Let us look at the material side, the art of preparing and constructing subtly devised arrangements of all kinds of materials as the basis of every culture of eating and indeed building.

[2] Rumohr, Karl Friedrich von: Geist der Kochkunst, Leipzig 1822; Reprint, Heidelberg 1994, p. 45

In his famous 1822 book *Geist der Kochkunst* ("The spirit of the art of cooking"), which is still worth reading, Karl Friedrich von Rumohr defines the art of cookery as follows: "The art of cooking develops, in natural materials that are at all suitable for nourishing or refreshing, their nutritious, reviving and delightful quality through fire, water and salt. Hence the famous saying by Horace recommending that usefulness should be mixed with grace ('omne tulit punctum qui miscuit utile dulci') should be applied only to cooking."[2]

This "recipe" for Horace's poetry can be applied not only to cookery, but also to architecture. Horace's fellow-countryman and contemporary Vitruvius defined its essential qualities with the trio *firmitas* (solidity), *utilitas* (usefulness) and *venustas* (grace). This harmonious triad of equally ranked qualities forming a unity as requirements for good architecture remains valid to the present day, as architecture is still about fitting solid materials together to create a stable, practical and handsome building. But the concepts can just as well be applied to cooking.

Firmitas (solidity) refers to handling materials correctly, which starts at the point when they are chosen. Vitruvius felt that meanness was a great mistake. The choice of the correct technique when working with materials is also an essential requirement if solidity and durability are to be guaranteed. Architecture and cooking start with knowledge about the quality of raw materials and mastering appropriate ways of processing or preparing them.

Utilitas, arranging spaces correctly, refers to the usefulness of that arrangement and the utility value of the building, which considerably affects the health and well-being of the people who live in it. In terms of cooking, nutritional value and the digestibility of the materials prepared could be mentioned in this context.

And finally *venustas*, grace, means a pleasing, appealing appearance as the product's aesthetic quality, the way it addresses our senses. Parallels in terms of architectural theory that could correspond to that Vitruvian trio of concepts can also be detected in Rumohr's writing, for example when he says: "Cookery makes itself useful by ceaselessly pursuing the lasting purpose of eating, nourishing and refreshing. But it has two ways of producing the delightful; first by following the above-mentioned purpose, for all nourishing and healthy foods usually taste good as well; then by" – and this could correspond with the function of ornament in architecture – "adding a suitable spice to merely nourishing dishes and foods, and at the same time lending them a pleasing appearance."[3]

[3] Ibid

[4] Original quotation: "...einen befriedigenden, sozusagen sättigenden Anblick..." in: Hegel, Georg Friedrich Wilhelm: Ästhetik, Frankfurt am Main, n. y., vol. 2, chapter 2, p.62

Here the interaction of the sensual manifestations of appearance, consistency, aroma and taste is addressed as a whole. Everyone knows that food must also appeal to the eye, or the eye eats as well – *das Auge isst mit* – as the German phrase has it. This statement also applies to architecture, which is not built primarily to be looked at, but the eye is again always invited to the table. All the visual arts produce food for the eye, and architecture, which creates a complementary environment to nature with its bodies of structure and space, does this especially. Leon Battista Alberti will have felt similarly about it. As a Renaissance man who took a sensual delight in things, he described looking at beautiful buildings in his 1485 book *De re aedificatoria* (Book 9, chapter 8) in a way that suggests the eye absolutely devouring its object, with apparently infinite passion. Georg Friedrich Wilhelm Hegel actually did treat architecture as a matter of feasting the eye in his "Aesthetics," which inspired him to come up with the excellent formulation that Greek temples offered "a satisfying, as it were satiating appearance,"[4] this in contrast with Gothic buildings, whose bony thinness obviously had little of substance to offer as food for the eye, so that one left the table hungry. Whatever would someone like Hegel have said about the decidedly fleshless fare offered by 20th century Modernism's "skin and bones buildings" (Mies van der Rohe)? Risking a further step forward on this philosophical, metaphorical plane, one could ask whether perhaps we owe the invention of the "filling trimmings" served with modern cuisine to the minimalist direction taken by cooking in the starving aridity of modern skeleton architecture?

Substance is the theme of cooking and of architecture. All craft techniques, including those of architecture, derive from awareness of the qualities and potential of the material and an appropriate way of treating it. Are things not very much the same when preparing a nourishing and tasty meal? An effort has to be made to establish the potential and characteristics of the material and thus to impose a sense of design on their appearance. It is only in this way that the material "as such" becomes material "for us," that it acquires "significance," i.e. it enters our world of ideas and evaluations. This is how it acquires "content" and "salary," because we ascribe qualities of its "own" to it, "owned" qualities that we credit to its account as characteristic features. "Any material is worth only what we make of it." – This statement by Mies van der Rohe makes most sense in the kitchen! What entitles us to call these techniques an "art" is this particular perfection in deploying and mastering them, which involves not only craft skills developed over a long period of time, but also developing and shaping certain ideas of taste and custom, of combinations and proportions, which have proved their worth, become accepted and refined themselves as cultural forms and types over the course of history.

Viticulture is an almost exemplary demonstration of this set of laws. Real quality is not the result of some random approach, but of following principles, and it cannot just be invented and produced technically from one day to the next. It is not possible – to use another of Mies van der Rohe's statements – to invent a new architecture every Monday, though nowadays many architects seem to think it is. And it is equally impossible to ignore the collective taste memory and create and successfully market a new wine on a whim in a very short time. Unlike the food for the eye offered by architecture, the palate is spared the extreme offences to taste sometimes imposed by building. Modern winegrowers, unlike some architects who think themselves modern, know that their craft requires a long process of becoming involved in certain "natural" conditions and that it means developing, adjusting and fine-tuning ideas of "taste," or let us rather say aesthetics. This is why every great wine can in its own way quite incidentally tell the palate and nose that have learned to refine their range of taste a story of cultivated "construction" as well; a story – as Heidegger would say – of tending, cherishing and caring for the earth.

Culture is a sediment of customs that have become habitual through long use, and at the same time are subject to a continual process of change and refinement that probably includes coincidences, but nothing random. In terms of cultural history it is certainly no coincidence that on the art-historical map of Europe the regions where architecture and the arts flourished mightily are usually the same as those where the cuisine is good, and wine is also made. Kitchen and cellar guarantee cultivated domesticity and sociable culture. The other arts also emerged from the context of private life and the domestic centre of dwelling, something we have almost forgotten as we are used to seeing works of art mainly in pure art spaces against the white and neutral wall of a museum.

Vineyard near Malans, the Grisons

No other architect and architectural theoretician has been as convinced as Gottfried Semper of the ardent interplay of all the fine arts and their communal origin in direct human need. Driven by this understanding of the cultural unity of art and life and passionately interested in raising the sense of art in general, he studied the patterns of building from a cultural and historical point of view like no other. He attended to building's technical requirements in terms of materials and processes to an unparalleled extent, thoroughly and in detail, starting with everyday things like dressing and household goods and vessels for storing things, then on to the actual spatial vessel that is a building, intended to "store" people. His intention was effectively to examine the whole "household" of the arts in the context of life, so that he would be able to explain the cultural-historical phenomenon of the emergence of formal principles and the formation of "styles" in the spirit of a "practical aesthetic."

Semper contributed indirectly to the comparability of cooking and architecture. In his 1851 essay *Die vier Elemente der Baukunst* ("The Four Elements of Architecture") he defined the fireplace as the "first element" of architecture. The hearth is the sacred centre and that causal first element, to protect which the other three space-defining elements, floor, wall and ceiling, are assembled in sequence. The domestic hearth is a "place" for living in Heidegger's sense, which collects and assembles, and thus triggers the creation and fitting together of spaces. The hearth is not just the practical and functional centre of the house, but also its cultic and sacred centre. Customs and traditions come into being around the hearth, which is why Semper also speaks of the hearth as the "moral element" of architecture; he also calls it the "embryo" of architecture. To this extent one could with some justification speak of the kitchen as architecture's womb and nursery.

In a similar way, but with other intentions, Andrea Palladio argued that architecture originated from the womb of dwelling. Palladio justified transferring the temple motif to the home, the "trade mark" of his architecture, as a quasi natural return of a sacred motif to the secular sphere, pointing out that in terms of the history of development the home preceded the temple, and imbued it with form, just as the hearth also preceded the altar. The fact that the hearth still serves us as a symbolic designation for an original centre is revealed by German language when we talk about an *Unruheherd* (trouble spot). Semper's friend Richard Wagner even spoke of the orchestra as the *technischer Herd* (technical hearth) for the preparation of his music drama.

Fire is also mentioned as the force creating civilisation by Vitruvius, the author of the oldest written text on architectural theory, in the so-called "legend of the origin of architecture" (book 2, chapter 1). We owe the origin of architecture and language to it. It is only the fireplace that ties people to a particular place and makes them settle there; this placing led to assembly, i.e. society, which also gave rise to the need for communication and for permanent housing. Interestingly enough, Vitruvius is thus suggesting that language and architecture emerged simultaneously as cultural phenomena as a consequence of man's being fixed in a particular place. As an institution, the hearth fixes man's thermal and social community, and thus creates architectural form. And this in its turn, as Adolf Behne put it so trenchantly in *The Modern Functional Building* ("Der moderne Zweckbau", 1926), is the key requirement for community and thus an eminently social matter: "Form is nothing more than the consequence of establishing a relationship between human beings. For the isolated or unique figure in nature there is no problem of form. The isolated figure, even in nature, is free. The problem of form arises when a collective is demanded. Form is the prerequisite under which a collective becomes possible."[5]

The hearth creates the firm connection with the place. Being tied to a place is, as we know, a prerequisite of both architecture and cooking. Building forms and eating habits develop on the spot, influenced by the conditions of heaven and earth, by the climate and the world of plants and animals. But cultural customs and habits come into being around this central point: what is customary (*das Gewohnte*) grows out of dwelling (*Wohnen*), as Nietzsche's incomparably poetic formulation in the 1883 *Posthumous Fragments* ("Nachgelassene Fragmente") explains: "What dwells around you, that you will soon make your custom: the customary arises from it. And where one sits for a long time, there the seated customs grow."[6] A more beautiful line has scarcely been written in the field of cultural history and architectural theory. Martin Heidegger could have used it as an introductory motto for his 1951 *Building, Dwelling, Thinking*.

Essentially little has changed to the present day in the cultural-historical significance of the fireplace as hearth and altar, as the warming and also the sacred, cultic centre of the home, even though the television has now taken over the function of the ritual centre of modern domesticity in many places. The candles we still like to put on our tables to give a meal a sense of solemnity are perhaps also nothing other than a cultural-historical reflection of that early historical starting-point from which the relationship between cooking and architecture stems. Ultimately both arts prepare a good proportion of their materials on fires. What would building be without ceramics and metallurgy, without bricks from a kiln and "hard-boiled" steel.

Gottfried Semper, often reprimanded as a materialist by the numerous people who misunderstand him, set off with almost Goethean universality down the long road from material via functions to the idea of form, and worked his way through the categories of materials, the techniques for working with them and the formal laws that apply to them. The logic of overcoming matter through an idea, and material through form, could hardly have been pronounced more radically by an alleged materialist. According to Semper the "destruction of material," in other words causing material to be forgotten or eliminated in favour of a purely aesthetic effect is the intention of all art. Are not cooking and eating also an act of enhancing and "destroying" material with great relish by artful preparation and consciously celebrated consumption?

The senses celebrate their own feast in this act of cultural "destruction," in order to cultivate delight in what can be seen, heard, tasted etc. in an "object," in the work of art, specially created for those senses. This enjoyment of enjoyment, or consumption, which confirms humans to be beings who both create and enjoy, or consume, is the basis of the cultural act that sees "material" as a means to achieving a higher, spiritual joy, and therefore conquers it. So transcending the material certainly does not bypass the material, quite the opposite, it passes through it, in full awareness of its quality and dignity. Thus

[5] Behne, Adolf: The Modern Functional Building, Santa Monica 1996, p. 137, (Der Moderne Zweckbau, Munich 1926, p. 59)

[6] Original quotation: "... was um euch wohnt, das wohnt sich bald euch an: Gewöhnung wird daraus. Und wo man lange sitzt, da wachsen Sitten." in: Nietzsche, Friedrich: Sämtliche Werke. Kritische Studienausgabe, ed. by Georgi Colli and Mazzino Montinari, Munich/Berlin/New York 1980, vol. 10, p. 631.

material and idea form a dialectical pair in an integrated process: just as the material unconsciously affects the form, it is the form that enables the material to make a conscious effect. So that act of transcendence succeeds only if the struggle between form and material leaves form as the victor, in other words it does not remain in the clutches of the material, but can handle it commandingly. This "complete mastery," to quote Semper, i.e. complete control of the material through technical ability to handle it and creative formal imagination, is the essential prerequisite for transforming aesthetic perception into a fully formed spiritual event.

The material has to be prepared skilfully for the purposes of this meeting of individual and object, as strictly speaking material is only another word for preparation. Building materials and nutritional materials are not simply given. The material must first of all be recognised, won over, as material, and tested against a particular intention in order to get an idea of its potential and what it "can" do. Conscious culinary enjoyment regularly produces surprises about the elementary combinations and technical procedures that allow everyday, familiar foodstuffs to be transformed into unbelievable, or shall we say untasted modes of expression in the hands of a real kitchen artist. The "preparation," as an act of refining nature, makes the raw material into "artistic material": stone is made into slabs, clay baked for bricks, wood is sawn up into beams and planks; in short, material is always a result of work, and to that extent already an artificial product, like the grape, which has to be tended and cared for even in the vineyard according to all the rules of art, in order to grant the wine a certain quality in terms of its "raw materials." Something similar also applies to other natural foodstuffs and material to be enjoyed by consumption.

An eye trained to be aware of the sensual quality of the material, and therefore critical, like a spoilt palate, cannot be so quickly fobbed off with a cheap deception, with visual "fast food," as it were; the eye that is also at the architectural table needs its nourishment to be prepared with refined artistry, in other words following an art of producing credible surfaces that are "tasteful" visually and also to the touch, an art that operates at the highest technical level. The art of satisfying the eye's desire through forms and surfaces, and thus also occupying reflective reason, needs an effort in terms of technique and imagination, as human beings want, as Carl Philip Moritz once so trenchantly put it in the late 18th century, "not just to take pleasure in dwelling in a building – they also want to take pleasure in looking at it – and" he adds a sentence that applies equally to cooking "just as many hands work to feed the eye as to nourish the body."[7]

[7] Moritz, Carl Philip: Vorbegriffe zu einer Theorie der Ornamente, Berlin 1793; Reprint, Nördlingen 1986, p. 4.

56

Architecture, as an art that is both necessary for our existence and at the same time beautiful, is not only food for the eye, but feeds – because it includes the other senses completely in experiencing it – the whole body, as it were. Demanding nourishment for the eye as a "gastronomic" element of architecture is certainly justified, so long as we do not forget that the eye does not exist in isolation, but is one organ in a body equipped with another four senses. The architecture of functionalism wanted to raise utility value to the rank of a formal statement. Thus the sign function as an essential function of architecture was suppressed, and its aesthetic impoverishment put in train. At the present time we are experiencing a hegemony of the visual in the media age, and this is going too far in the opposite direction. Architecture seems to be so in love with the media image that physical experience of the substance of the building flees into the virtual, and utility value as opposed to the sensation value of visual effects that wear off increasingly rapidly is sometimes completely neglected.

Cooking seems to me to be good training in how food for the eye and feeding the whole body can be brought into a harmonious relationship. Architecture begins, as has already been said, with fire, with the hearth, as its first element. Cooking as the art of putting ingredients together to make a nourishing and appetising whole, it could be said conversely, is also to be seen as an activity involving design and architecture on a small scale. Can one really understand anything about home life without having cooked, or at least having tried? Because architecture starts with fire, the architect can also go to school in the kitchen. Something essentially real can definitely be learned within its four walls.

Modernism made the kitchen into a one-man factory for preparing foodstuffs, under the banner of progress and in the name of a heroically constituted new man. The hearth fell victim to the renunciation of domesticity. In extreme cases, cooking was banished into the corner "kitchenette," like being made to stand in the corner as a punishment. The resocialisation of the modern kitchen isolated from family life took place a long time ago. Bringing back functions that once placed the living-kitchen at the heart of the living experience is part of better housing construction, and postmodern design stages all variants of the aestheticisation of the kitchen, making it a full part of home life. The great success of television cookery programmes proves that the homely hearth and the kitchen are waiting to be rediscovered as the workshop for a life culture of "slow food."

57

Vitruvius Teutsch. *Nemlichen des aller namhafftigsten und hocherfarnesten Römischen Architecti und Kunstreichen Werck oder Bawmeisters Marci Vitruvij Pollionis Zehen Bücher von der Architectur und künstlichen Bawen... Erstmals verteutscht und in Truck verordnet Durch Gualtherum Hermenium Rivium Medi. & Math. Vormals in Teutsche sprach zu tranferiren noch von niemand sonst unterstanden sonder fur unmüglichen geachtet worden*, Nuremberg 1548, p. LXI

The two principles of ambitious modern cuisine, which Rumohr formulated as things to be taken for granted as early as 1822, were enough at first in both architecture and cooking to achieve a basic gourmet status in terms of the craft. And that is first to develop a sense of the quality of the basic foodstuffs and the freshness of the products, and to leave out anything that has been chemically faked, conserved, improperly bred. In the building "market" such basic foodstuffs certainly do not include synthetic products like thermal skin, plastic windows etc. Secondly, one would be able to learn to restrict oneself to using the basic elements of the craft, and not to adulterate the taste of the cooked food by over-frying or over-boiling, or with the wrong ingredients, accompaniments and sauces. On the architectural side one could perhaps draw parallels with the effect of material quality, tectonic sensibility and unadulterated, i.e. credible surfaces.

And finally, as far as ingredients and accompaniments are concerned, it is of course not enough here in the long run simply to leave things out. The barrenness of modern architecture should have opened even the last modernist's eyes to the fact that ornament is not a "crime." Precisely because there must be eye-appeal as well, it is probably right to decorate a building. But it must be remembered that the ornament is not there to satiate the eye, but to emphasise and refine the flavour. August Welby Pugin's famous saying applies to the art of cooking and to the art of construction: "It is all right to decorate construction but never construct decoration."[8]

[8] Quoted from Venturi, Robert, Brown, Denise Scott and Izenour, Steven: Learning from Las Vegas, Cambridge, Mass. 1972.

Edouard Manet: Le Déjeuner sur l'herbe, 1863

59

Rules of Fasting and Desire Derailed
Notes on Architecture and Gastronomy
Stanislaus von Moos

One of the surprises at the major retrospective of Herzog and de Meuron's work shown in the Schaulager in the Emanuel Hoffmann-Stiftung in Basel in spring 2004 was a large dark red "sugar object" displayed on a table-top. It turned out to be a tub of hard, glass-clear molasses with a large number of stalagmites rising from it like a fountain, vaguely reminiscent of Henry van de Velde's architectural forms or certain details in the nearby Goetheanum in Dornach. Making this object must have cost a considerable effort – the individual, often adventurously fragile forms were obviously produced by dripping and then raised to an upright position after cooling.

Herzog & de Meuron Architekten: Sugar Object, 2004

If one looks around contemporary artists' work and writings, this work of art in edible materials – a homage to the artist Dieter Roth's chocolate objects, which were shown a few months earlier in the same museum – is not an isolated case. Architects increasingly seem to be looking for new processes for endowing their work with form in the border regions of art and cooking, not least so that they can then translate these into the language of computer-controlled processes – Frank O. Gehry or Greg Lynn[1] are both examples here. Of course such trans-disciplinary cross-pollinations between gastronomy and architecture are by no means new. There are countless pieces of evidence for the fact that there have always been structural links between kitchen and building site, menu and building project, and that these links trigger certain thought processes or at least encourage particular lines of argument. The following advice to his colleagues, composed as early as 1862 by the English architect James Ferguson is one of the most artful of them: "The process by which a hut to shelter an image is refined into a temple, or a meeting house into a cathedral, is the same as that which refines a boiled neck of mutton into *côtelettes à l'Impériale* or a grilled fowl into *Poulet à la Marengo*. So essentially is this the case, that if you wish to acquire a knowledge of the true principle of design in architecture you will do better to study the works of Soyer or Mrs Glass than any or all of the writers on architecture from Vitruvius to Pugin." Peter Collins, from whose book *Changing Ideals in Modern Architecture, 1750-1950* (published in 1964) the quotation is taken, adds that it is astonishing that no other architectural theorist has drawn on the "gastronomic analogy" for architectural theory – and this all the more so as the concept of "aesthetics," which was widespread in the 17th and 18th centuries, is based directly on the notion of "taste" – in other words all the more so as aesthetic perception derives directly from the experience of tasting and consuming food.[2]

The following contribution to the discussion is essentially nothing more than an inflated footnote to the remark by Collins that has just been quoted. In fact when Collins asserts that Ferguson was the only 19th century architect who was interested in the relationship between architecture and gastronomy, it should be remembered that in contrast with this, corresponding attempts appear extremely frequently in the 20th century. Of course, as in other fields as well, eating metaphors in architectural discourse frequently exhaust themselves in a rhetorical function in service of the *captatio benevolentiae* or of a paradox to arouse interest. And beyond this, they also serve the purpose of awakening sympathy in an audience that has remained unfreighted with expertise for fundamental ideas about things like function, efficiency and performance in building – but also about decency, taste, tradition or change, erosion of form, prestige and play in architecture. Certainly these rhetorical ancillary functions in gastronomy would not be worthy of further mention in the architecture discourse, if a certain complicity between kitchen and building site inherent in the matter itself did not emerge: a more deeply rooted analogy in the way nature is appropriated and transformed in both fields.

Both fields, i.e. preparing and consuming food and producing and using habitable space, are about organising sensual perception and aesthetic pleasure intelligently – and ultimately also about sheer survival, about life and death. If you don't eat, you die. And you die if you are left exposed to the elements without protection.

Functionalistic entreaty for abstinence

For long periods, modern 20th century architecture placed itself under a puritanical, indeed almost masochistic insistence on abstinence. This may seem far-fetched, but it is supported by presenting some examples, however fragmentary, of the stereotypical "rules of fasting" or at least "appeals for moderation" proclaimed by its ideologies. Eclectic 19th century architecture, or of the present day and, absolutely all of "Postmodernism" are particularly popular victims of functionalistic invocations of abstinence. Addressing this Kenneth Frampton sums it up in a way when he postulates that it is certainly one of an architect's duties to serve "living needs," but never the seamy side of "desire," which is only semi-conscious.[3]

But it seems that this was precisely the strategy of historicism (and not just historicism, but more of that later). And where were these lived out more authentically than in the palace hotels of the Belle Epoque? Jacques Gubler suggests in this context that one of the qualities of late 19th century hotel architecture is that it should charm the senses, and should do this by constantly introducing new effects. This is essentially nothing other than the purpose of cookery – to the extent that all its works pursue the aim of titillating the palate with the greatest possible degree of variety. To support his case, he shows a cake for a special occasion which is a copy of the *Hotel des Avants'* guesthouses above Montreux on Lake Geneva (the Villa Pappazoglu).[4] In fact the short circuit from historical architecture to cookery here is revealing, as architecture of this kind does not just look like a wedding cake, – it actually is one.

[1] Lynn, Greg: Architectural Curvilinearity. The Folded, the Pliant, and the Supple, in: Architectural Design (special issue on "Folding in Architecture"), 1993, no. 3-4, p. 8; see Paulette Singley and Jamie Horwitz: Introduction, in same author, (ed.): Eating Architecture, Cambridge, MA/ London (MIT Press), 2004, pp. 5-17
My own interest in the subject of "gastronomy" goes back to a study of design history in Switzerland (Industrieästhetik. Ars Helvetica, vol. XI, Disentis, 1992, s. pp. 71-90). I have Paul Hugger to thank for some valuable ideas; he carried out a teaching event with me at the University of Zurich (1991/92). The above-mentioned anthology by Jamie Horwitz and Paulette Singley did not appear until after the reading of the present text at Kloster Eberbach and proved indispensable for sharpening my thinking on the subject. To my shame it was there I first found the important essay by Marco Frascari already published in 1986: Semiotica ab Edendo. Taste in Architecture, ibid., pp. 191-203.

[2] Collins, Peter: Changing Ideals in Modern Architecture. 1750-1950, Montreal (McGill University Press), 1965, p. 167

[3] Frampton, Kenneth: Introduction. The Work of Architecture in the Age of Commodification, in: William Saunders (ed.), Commodification and Spectacle in Architecture, Minneapolis (University of Minnesota Press), 2005, pp. ix-xviii

[4] Gubler, Jacques: Les identités d'une région, in: werk-archithese, 1977, no. 6, 1977, pp. 3-11

61

[5] Meyer, Peter: Kochkunst und andere Künste, in: Das Werk, 1930, no. 7, pp. 216-218

[6] Gregotti, Vittorio: Editoriale, in: Rassegna (Minimal), 1979, no. 36, pp. 4-7

In 1930 another architectural theoretician, Peter Meyer, then editor of the Swiss architecture magazine *Das Werk*, made the following remarks about a cookery exhibition mounted as part of the ZIKA in Zurich: "It really seems the ambition of culinary artists of this decorative persuasion to prepare food in such a way that it looks like artistic dummies, like lacquered plaster. (…) These culinary artists go to work with bitter seriousness, with a tragic lack of humour, attempting to remove any suggestion of being appetising from their food, to denature it, to use art to make it untouchable."[5] Of course Meyer's target here is not really the "culinary artists" of 1930, but the architects of the 19th century, or their successors in the present day – architects and

The "Villa Pappazoglu" as a feast-day cake (photograph, Christmas 1903). The "Villa Pappazoglu" is the guest-house serving the Hotel des Avants near Montreux, built in 1898.

interior designers, in other words, who continue to affect this denaturing treatment of materials and forms that so effectively threw the elite exponents of preserving regional and local character in the early years of the century off course.

Different (and essentially analogous) Vittorio Gregotti: Arguing half a century later, he directs his attack on *patisserie* unambiguously at the immediate present. He wonders about the increasing formal "complexity" in more recent (in this case Postmodern) architecture, about the character of the eclectic montage that characterises so many buildings in recent years (in an editorial for a number on "Minimalism" in the magazine he edited, *Rassegna*, no. 36): "Without wishing to insult the art of *patisserie*, it has to be said that these ideas frequently exude an all-pervading aroma of cake, as if to put the finishing touches to the glaze of optimism that surrounds them …"[6] We can only speculate about which colleagues Gregotti can have been thinking of …

Some little time before Meyer and Gregotti, Le Corbusier had allowed himself to be tempted to some particularly shrill remarks about *haute cuisine* and *patisserie*. In fact, in contrast with Le Corbusier's boastful fulminations, both Meyer and Gregotti cultivate a positively lofty style. Le Corbusier felt that the academic architecture of his day was the apotheosis of adulteration and unproductive, mind-deadening gluttony – something for which, in his opinion, a certain Brillat-Savarin had written the relevant rules (Le Corbusier's example to end all examples is the Palace of the League of Nations in Geneva, completed in 1937, a building for which he had himself submitted a competition design ten years previously, which admittedly had been rejected): "We have had enough of this Brillat-Savarin: Cuisine for diplomatic dinners and lunches, where black tie and uniform (à la 'Général de la Grande Armée') are obligatory. One takes leeks, asparagus, potatoes, beef, butter, spices, fruit and, as a result of a science that has spawned entire books, everything is adulterated, everything is neutralised so that it tastes the same. The only result of all this is that one has successfully so overloaded stomachs with the wines and stinking cheese that the head can no longer function. And that at the

Michael Graves: Disneyworld, Orlando, FL. "Swans Hotel", 1984

very moment when business has to be discussed: when there are negotiations about war and peace to conduct, about alliances, customs duties, countless speculations. Like snakes, one digests the countless dangerous combinations of a world that in reality has ceased to exist."

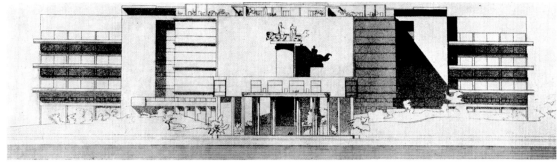

Grande Salle des Assemblées. La vue du Lac

Le Corbusier and Pierre Jeanneret: Palace for the League of Nations in Geneva. Elevation of the show façade of the plenary chamber facing the lake, competition project dating from 1926

And now comes the leap into architecture: "That is precisely the point that architecture has reached. The academic palaces of Geneva were the most unimaginable canopies of red plush and gilded silk ribbon that one can imagine. This palace had one clear function: handling work for the world's best benefit, just as a meal also has a clear function: to nourish the organism. Where do you think you are going! Working, hurrying, clear and concise, precise? And what then happens to diplomacy? And where is architecture's culinary taste going?" (…) "Hand on heart: this taste of international hotel cuisine with this Brillat-Savarin sauce and its indigestible truffled *pâté de foie gras*, do they even bring to their own minds the jaundice of the Salons des Artistes Français?"[7] The following has to be added here: The book *Physiologie du goût*, by the lawyer, historian and amateur physiologist Brillat-Savarin, is one of the key guidelines to gastronomy published in the 19th century – along with the work called *Geist der Kochkunst* ("The Spirit of Gastronomy") written by the art historian Carl Friedrich von Rumohr, which systematically examined the cross connections between cookery and fine art for the first time.[8] And as one would expect, Le Corbusier's tirades against Brillat-Savarin fall far short of the target – and by doing that they provide a glimpse of one of the modern gastronomy discourse's stereotypical schemes of thought. Jean-François Rével called it the masochists' scheme of thought; he seems to be branding roughly all modern civilisation's signs of decay (from colonialism via bourgeois bad taste to the gentrification of the proletariat) with his suspicion of the "unduly complicated" rules of classical cuisine.[9] Le Corbusier said of his own design for the League of Nations building : "This palace had one clear function: handling work for the world's best benefit …" No wonder then if this "palace" is more oriented towards a factory building than Versailles, that the factory-like exterior is compellingly derived from the need to find a pictorial language appropriate to the function of this "working building" – a building that has an unambiguously "productive" function: "working, hurrying, lucid and concise, precise …, just as a meal also has a clear function: to nourish the organism."[10] All in all: *Werkzeug* (lit.: tool) rather than *Schleckzeug* (lit.: a titbit to lick at) – that is how Le Corbusier could have summed it up if he had been writing in German. Max Bill, who was a little younger, did it for him instead.[11]

The logic of "variety"

Le Corbusier's tirade against Brillat-Savarin is perhaps no more than an angry mixture of puritanical excess of zeal and superficial gastronomic knowledge. His writings also contain much more useful approaches to thinking about the subject of gastronomy. One example is the remarkable "menu" Le Corbusier used in 1924 to compile a selection of "manières de penser à l'urbanisme," in the form of a selection of city views. What seems at a first glance like a typology of the urban turns out on closer examination to be an improvised catalogue of graphic forms of representation for cities. The upper part contains two rapidly jotted "impressions" (in the first section Pera, then Istanbul, seen from the Bosporus). Then – in the middle – a typological inventory (Rome) and, at the bottom, a drawn copy of a historical veduta (Sienna).

[7] Le Corbusier: Précisions sur un état présent de l'architecture et de l'urbanisme, Paris (Vincent Fréal), 1930 (1969 edition), p. 11f.

[8] Rumohr, Karl Friedrich von: Geist der Kochkunst, Heidelberg (Manutius Verlag), 1994 (first ed. 1822)

[9] Rével, Jean-François: Brillat-Savarin ou le style aimable, in: Brillat-Savarin: Physiologie du goût, Paris (Flammarion), 1982, pp. 5-15

[10] Le Corbusier: Précisions, op.cit.
[11] A chapter on American Streamline Design in Max Bill: Form. A survey of formal development around the mid XX century, Basel (Werner), 1952, carries the title "Vom Werkzeug zum Schleckzeug" (Eng.: From Making to Faking; Fr. De l'outil à la sucrerie), p. 46ff

Le Corbusier: *Classement et choix*. Illustration from *L'Esprit nouveau* no. 21, showing four Genres depicting historical cities

[12] Le Corbusier: Classement et choix, in: Esprit Nouveau, no.21, reprinted in same author: Urbanisme, Paris (Crès), 1925, p. 57. For a more detailed discussion of this "menu" see: Stanislaus von Moos: Voyages en Zigzag, in same author and Arthur Rüegg (eds.) Le Corbusier Before Le Corbusier, New Haven/London (Yale University Press), 2002, pp. 22-43

Some headwords in the margins serve to give the "table" the character to a systematic presentation. The point is the link between the "character" of the places shown each time and the form of presentation chosen from case to case – word for word:

"Pera: The saw blade of a city of merchants, pirates and golddiggers

Istanbul: The ardour of the minarets, the calm of Allah's shallow domes, watchful, yet oriental and unapproachable

Rome: Geometry, remorseless order, war, civilisation, organisation

Sienna: The fear-ridden tumult of the Middle Ages. Hell and Heaven in one."[12]

The four sketches that make up the catalogue – actually city-branding *avant la lettre* – date from 1911-14. They stand for four *modi* or drawing *genres* and as such are typical of the kind of material art school graduates in the early 20th century were supplied with so that they would be up to coping with historical monuments and landscapes on their travels.

What has all that to do with gastronomy? – Casually, but unmistakably, the catalogue of graphic headlines is related to the culture of eating: "Just as the palate can taste the variety of a well-composed menu, our eyes are also tuned to well-organised joys."[13] We have got it: gastronomy is about variety – whereas in art and architecture the key is "well-organised joys." (As far as the first thesis is concerned, it must owe more to Brillat-Savarin than Le Corbusier seems to realise.) So it seems ultimately to be about cementing the contrast between the culture of the menu (= variable and diverse) and the culture of architectural form (= simple and unambiguous). But listen: Le Corbusier would not be Le Corbusier if he were not able to play on both instruments precisely as an architect – that of classical purity and that of *variété*: "There is a certain relationship between quality and quantity, which makes the functions fit together. One should not always rub the eye in the same direction; it will tire if we do. Take care that there is the variety ("assolements") in the spectacle needed for the *promenade* to take place without people getting tired or becoming sleepy."[14] The key word here is *promenade* and the intended principle is that of the *promenade architecturale* as the medium of a sequential acknowledgement of vedutas in chronological order as cities are walked through and – above all – individual

Le Corbusier and Pierre Jeanneret: Villa La Roche-Jeanneret in Paris, 1924
View into the hall

buildings, for: "Behind the eye is this mobile and generous, fertile, imaginative, logical and noble thing: the mind. (…) What the eye will place in before it will trigger a condition of joy."[15] The gourmet's *flânerie* through the seductive landscapes of a sophisticated menu is, seen like this, anything but fundamentally different from that of a visitor who is initiated in the secrets of architecture and art strolling through the villa of the La Roche art collector in Paris – that building that first put the logic of the *promenade architecturale* into operation as a programme for the first time.

Surrealism and aesthetics of convulsion

Until the most recent past, Salvador Dalí was much more in the public eye as a painter than because of his extravagant architectural ambitions. But it is precisely these that turn out in the present context to be "just the feast we were waiting for."[16]

Dalí made a not inconsiderable effort to be acknowledged (at least by his own circle of fans) as Le Corbusier's great opponent, that is as proclaiming an alternative to architectural functionalism. Dalí's fierce partisanship vis-à-vis art nouveau is to be understood in this light, and especially his "scandalous" enthusiasm for the Catalan architect Antoni Gaudí – scandalous to the extent that the functionalist architectural avant-garde of the 1920s were scarcely able to see this architect as anything other than a derailment caused by misguided artistic desire. Even more clearly than for Le Corbusier, for Dalí "eating," or gastronomy (the science of the stomach) was the set parameter for sensual experience. "La beauté sera comestible ou ne sera pas," he wrote in 1933 – an obvious parody of André Breton's motto "la beauté sera convulsive."[17] Art nouveau architecture, he argues, embodies both the most concrete *and* the craziest form of hyper-materialism: "An illustration of the apparent paradox can be found in a comparison that is often deployed, frequently with the intention to mislead, but is still so lucid: in comparing an art nouveau building with a cake, an exhibitionistic and ornamental piece of *confiserie*."[18]

He goes on to say that when art nouveau is juxtaposed with *confiserie*, this is a comparison that is as "lucid as it is intelligent: not just because it is attacking the violently materialistic prosaic quality of the 'immediate needs' on which ideal needs are based, but because in this way, which is very real and free of euphemisms, the nutritive, edible character of buildings of this kind is being pointed out, which in fact are nothing other than the first edible buildings, and so also the first and only buildings that can be eroticised, whose mere existence proves the amorous notion of this function that is as urgent as it is essential, which consists of really being able to eat the object of desire."[19] If in these lines, which seem to have been written in delirium, Dalí is attacking what he himself calls the "violently materialistic prosaic quality of the 'immediate needs'", he is doing it via a digression on regressing in childlike narcissism – i.e. that stage of a child's development where objects are judged above all from the point of view of their suitability for oral consumption. Here, it is implied, is the root of sensual pleasure – and having rediscovered this root is Gaudí's lasting achievement. That is what puts him ahead of the metastases of "functionality."[20]

[13] Le Corbusier: Urbanisme, op.cit., p. 56

[14] Ibid., p. 56f.

[15] Ibid., p. 58
Working on the basis of Colin Rowe's and Bernhard Hoesli's ideas, Jamie Horwitz and Paulette Singley remember that architecture and gastronomy also interact directly in Le Corbusier's concrete design practice. Writing about Le Corbusier's still life painting, they say: "…one might hazard the assertion that for modern architecture and urbanism the production of architecture moved from the tabletop – loaded with its scattered debris of crockery and foodstuffs – to the canvas without ever having looked at the site" (Introduction, in: Eating Architecture, op. cit., p. 17). Following George Hersey, they locate the conditions fort his analogy in the world of cult.

[16] For the problem field of "Dalí and architecture," see sources including: Dalí Arquitectura, Barcelona (Fundacio Caixa de Catalunya/ Fundacio Gala-Salvador Dalí), 1996; Montse Aguer, Félix Fanés and Juan-José Lahuerta (eds.): Dalí, Salvador. Dream of Venus (Fundacio "La Caixa"/Fundaciò Gala Salvador Dalí) Bonet, Llorenç: Gaudí / Dalí, Sabadell (H. Kliczkowski-Onlybook), 2002, and also Schaffner, Ingrid and Schaal, Eric: Salvador Dalí's Dream of Venus. The Surrealist Funhouse from the 1939 World's Fair, New York (Princeton Architectural Press), 1999. – For the field of tension Le Corbusier – Dalí see Lahuerta, Juan José: Decir ANTI es decir PRO. Escenas de la vanguardia en Espana, Teruel (Museo de Teruel), 1999

[17] Dalí, Salvador: De la beauté terrifiante et comestible de l"architecture Modern Style, in: Minotaure, 1933, nos. 3-4, pp. 69-76.; cf. also Dalí's later text on Guimard: Cylindrical Monarchy of Guimard, in: Arts Magazine, New York 1970, nos. 44:5, pp. 42-43

[18] "De la beauté terrifiante et comestible de l'architecture Modern Style", op.cit.

[19] Ibid.

[20] Frascari, S. Marco: Semiotica ab Edendo. Taste in Architecture, in Horwitz, J. u. P. S., Eating Architecture, Cambridge, MA (MIT Press), 2004, pp. 191-202 (first pub. 1986)

CONTRE LE FONCTIONNALISME IDÉALISTE, LE FONCTIONNEMENT SYMBOLIQUE-PSYCHIQUE-MATÉRIALISTE.

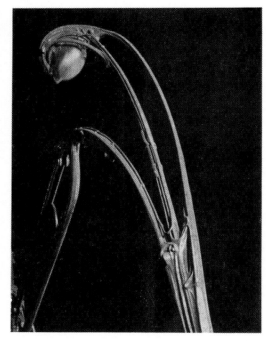

IL S'AGIT ENCORE D'UN ATAVISME MÉTALLIQUE DE L'ANGÉLUS DE MILLET.

MANGE-MOI !

MOI AUSSI

AVEZ-VOUS DÉJA VU L'ENTRÉE DU MÉTRO DE PARIS ?

Avez-vous déjà vu l'entrée du métro de Paris? ("Have you seen the entrance to the Paris Métro Yet?"). Picture accompanying Salvador Dalí's essay *De la beauté terrifiante et comestible de l'architecture Modern Style* ("On the terrible and edible beauty of art nouveau architecture") in the magazine *Minotaure*, 1933

Not that a psychoanalytical interpretation of the kind that Dalí is proposing here would exclude different, more obvious and also more banal approaches to the "edible character of buildings of this kind." Roughly along the lines of the idea that the "edibility" of such architecture indicates possibilities of "consuming" such objects in a way different from utilitarian use – e.g. as a mere sign, independently of its material function. As we consume "event architecture" – like for example the ghostly shooting-range magic of Dalí's own "Teatre Museu Dalí" in Figueres with its battlements in the shape of eggs and its façade patterning with rosette-shaped loaves of bread.

Figueres, Spain: Teatre-Museu Salvador Dalí. The Figueres municipal palace, rebuilt and decorated with giant eggs and loaves of bread, based on a project by Salvador Dalí, 1974

This museum which was established while Dalí was still alive and later entrusted to the use of his home town is one of those Modernist locations where artistic ambition and populist entertainment extend their hand to each other like will-o'-the-wisps. Partly a colossal art chamber, partly a commercial sale of artistic curiosities in the tradition of Surrealism and Symbolism, the institution speculates with the popular enthusiasm for eccentricity demonstrated with virtuosity, and as well as this offers a good deal of learned nonsense in the border area between reactionary polit-iconography and artistic subversion.[21] Those familiar with the Spanish cultural landscape will not miss the analogy with, for example, the patterned palace façade of the Casa de las Conchas in Salamanca – and according to their aesthetic preferences they will be annoyed by the reference to the symbol of Spanish monarchism (especially under the Franco regime) – or the mocking transformation of the royalist shells on the façade of the Casa de las Conchas into loaves of bread, or be delighted by the crowning of the palace façade with gigantic eggs, invoking physical fertility rather than reactionary political authority. For Dalí, bread is the symbol of nourishment par excellence, the "sacred food" – something that is "part of necessity in a tyrannical way," and that consequently can be freed from the tyranny of functionalistic thinking only by art.[22]

Dalí wrote his essay on art nouveau in 1933. Perhaps he was aware of Le Corbusier's recently published mockery of Brillat-Savarin. In this case, at least one trigger for his surrealistic fantasies about edible architecture would be in Le Corbusier's work. Only a little later, Dalí's functionalistic alter ego had again twisted the gastronomic analogy back into the negative in his own, Protestant way by comparing (in his book *Quand les cathédrales étaient blanches*, 1937) New York with a table that has not been cleared after a meal: "No one tidied up after the meal; the remains of a banquet whose guests have long since disappeared have been left in disarray: congealed sauces, bones and bits of fish, wine stains, breadcrumbs and the dirty cutlery and crockery in complete chaos."[23]

Surrealistic table fantasies recycled in a Postmodern way

Dalí's and Le Corbusier's frivolous invocations of food gave way to a more sober vocabulary in the architectural discourse of the neo- and late Modern post-war period. It was only Postmodernism that started to raise the convergences of cooking and building and the parallelisms of the olfactory and optical devouring of nature and artificiality among architects.

[21] Gimenez-Frontin, J.-L.: Teatre-Museu Dali, Madrid (Tisquets/Electa), 1994; 2001

[22] Dalí, Salvador: Das geheime Leben des Salvador Dalí, München (Schirmer-Mosel), 1984, p. 376; see also: Salvador Dalí 1904-1984, Stuttgart (Hatje), 1989, pp. 88 and 174

[23] Le Corbusier: Quand les cathédrales étaient blanches, Paris (Plon), 1937, Paris ed. (Gonthier), 1965, p. 7

[24] Venturi, Robert: Süss-Sauer. Eine Methode der vergleichenden Analyse und ein Entwurfsverfahren, die manieristische Dualität einbegreifen. Plädoyer für eine "neutrale" Architektur als Hintergrund für Ikonographie und elektronische Medien, in: archithese, no.6. 1995, pp. 6-12

For Frank O. Gehry, the Saturday carp – his grandmother is said always to have granted it a respite in the bathtub before committing it to the pan – became a formal paradigm, in fact almost a trademark. Gehry even presented a gigantic model of a building in the shape of a fish at the major Council of Europe exhibition in Genoa in 2004. Robert Venturi called one of his more recent manifestos – published in 1994 – "Sweet and Sour," and this helped a restaurant menu (in this case a Chinese restaurant menu) to make a recent appearance on the architectural stage. Venturi plays a key part in the context of the reintroduction of the gastronomic metaphor to Postmodern architectural discussion.[24] Even a quarter of a century before "Sweet and Sour" he had used a snack bar in the shape of a duck as an example to show how architectural sign languages emerge and work in the everyday world.

In Robert Venturi's example building, the duck occupies the opposite position to the decorated shed. This duck is the epitome of an architecture that embodies its function iconically, by its form – whereas the decorated shed is the epitome of a functional architecture of minimal signs whose function is presented merely graphically, using an applied sign. One has to be aware that Venturi's campaign is on behalf of the "decorated shed;" the duck stands for an out-of-date architectural practice for creating form. Thus two facts should be noted: one is that a duck-shaped grill bar of all things (in contrast, let us say, to a factory, an ocean liner or a grain silo) could become a visual catchword in Postmodern architectural discussion. On the other hand we have the fact that the catchword ultimately carries negative coding – similarly to Bill's *Schleckzeug* and Gregotti's *patisserie*. Thus the duck by the side of the road in Long Island, alongside all the other polemic implications of this example of popular *architecture parlante*, is two things at once: an unmistakable indication that in the age of Venturi and Gehry, the mythology of the Protestant work ethic that dominates functionalism has been replaced by a mythology of consumerism and hedonism, and by a final flicker of puritanical resistance to consumerism.

Something similar most certainly applies to the mural-size, but no less ambiguous travesty of Thomas Cole's "Dream of an architect," painted in 1820, which the Venturi, Scott Brown and Associates practice recently presented as part of its major retrospective in Philadelphia (2001). Admittedly, the polemic against consumerism seems to have been largely faded out here.

68

Robert Venturi: "Duck" and "Decorated Shed"
from *Learning from Las Vegas*, 1972

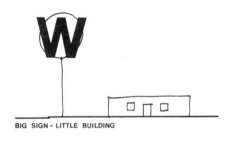

BIG SIGN - LITTLE BUILDING

OR

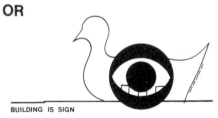

BUILDING IS SIGN

15. Big sign-little building or building as sign

An architect, resting on an enormous pedestal, is meditating about the heroic architectural landscape at his feet: a Gothic church, a classical Greek and an Egyptian temple and, rising above them, a pyramid – the collected inventory of sublime architectural languages, and there to be applied to 19th century monuments – so much for Cole's picture. The Venturis place a gigantic doughnut, as if as a joke, at the top of the panorama, seconded by an equally gigantic hot dog, overflowing with ketchup, flanking the neon façade of the Stardust Casino in Las Vegas. A warning to architects to keep a place in architecture for the surges of contemporary desire. And at the same time a somewhat alarming image of the times.

Robert Venturi, "Dream of an architect" (photo-montage based on the picture of the same name painted by Thomas Cole), 2001

Taste as a court of appeal

Brillat-Savarin coined the phrase *On devient cuisinier, mais on naît rôtissier* ("Cooks are made, but *rôtissiers* are born").[25] Auguste Perret translated this into architectural language as *On devient ingénieur, mais on naît architecte* ("Engineers are made, but architects are born").[26] The implication in each case is that perfection in the lower of the two art forms can be achieved by correct calculation, but in the higher one only by the ultimately incalculable factors of talent and experience. Both these things, talent and experience, are the irreplaceable requirements for "taste" as "a knowledge that does not know," as James Fergusson put it.[27]

In a theoretical statement they made in the 1980s, the Munich architects Heinz Hilmer and Christoph Sattler submitted a plea for architecture to return to the traditional area of validity of "taste" – just as taste had developed in the cuisine of preceding centuries. In other words, they mean that looking at (and using) architecture is subject to the same rules as tasting a dish, and quote Immanuel Kant in this context: "Taste is the ability to judge an object or a way of conceiving an idea by finding it pleasing, or not finding it pleasing, without any interest. The object of such a pleasing sensation is called beautiful."[28] With Immanuel Kant behind them, Hilmer & Sattler are making a conservative point – and not just within the spectrum of recent architecture (think of their Gemäldegalerie in Berlin, which picks up pre-Modern models so effortlessly, but also in the spec-

[25] Brillat-Savarin, Physiologie du goût, op.cit., p. 20

[26] Quoted from Frascari, Marco: Semiotioca ab Edendo, op.cit.

[27] Frascari, Marco, op.cit.

[28] translated by Michael Robinson; original German text: "Geschmack ist das Beurteilungsvermögen eines Gegenstandes oder einer Vorstellungsart durch ein Wohlgefallen, oder ein Missfallen, ohne alles Interesse. Der Gegenstand eines solchen Wohlgefallens heißt schön." Kant, Immanuel: Kritik der Urteilskraft, Wilhelm Weidschedel (ed.), Wiesbaden, 1974, S. 124; full English text in: Kant, Immanuel:Critique of Judgement, trans. James Creed Meredith, Oxford 1911. The corresponding statement by Hilmer & Sattler is to be found in: Baulig, Josef Walter: Geschichte und Rezeption. Theorien und Projekte: Heinz Hilmer & Christoph Sattler, Oswald Mathias Ungers, Johannes Uhl, (diss., unpubl.), 1986, p. 40

[29] Collins, Peter, op.cit., p. 169f

[30] "Le goût dépravé dans les arts est de se plaire à des sujets qui révoltent les esprits bien faits; de préférer le burlesque au noble, le précieux et l'affecté au beau simple et naturel: c'est une maladie de l'esprit." Voltaire: Goût, in: Diderot, Denis und d'Alembert, Jean le Rond (ed.): Encyclopédie ou dictionnaire raisonné, Paris, n.y.

trum of the current revival of the gastronomic analogy. They would presumably also agree with Peter Collins, who wrote: "The standards of gastronomy have remained unchanged for two centuries and are uncontested. The standards of architecture might also be uncontested if romantic influences had nor, for two centuries, vitiated its theoretical basis, and spread the germs of its debilitating criteria like phylloxera throughout the Western world. It is no coincidence (continues the Canadian Collins) that Anglo-Saxon cooking is proverbially bad, for bad food and bad architecture both derive from the same philosophical disease."[29] Collins thought he could conclude from this that the gastronomic anthology had been driven off course as a consequence of this romantic infection. He feels that "pleasing sensation" of which Kant spoke, derived from the principle of pleasing the palate, and thus in the broader sense from "taste," is relevant to the present as an architectural maxim. The fact is, he says, that Modern architecture did not address itself to the public, did not want to "please" – it was perhaps guided much more by the inherent rules of formal or constructive logic that are subject only marginally to the rules of finding something "pleasing."

That is how Collins saw it in 1967. I hope to have shown that the situation today, in the early 21st century, has changed strikingly – for better or for worse. We have before us the results of a slow shift of theoretical attention in architecture from the production aesthetic to the aesthetic of effect and reception – from the question of how the inner structure of architecture should be to the question of what architecture looks like, what impact it makes, how it "tastes." In the universe of global marketing these things count more that the monumentalisation of the Protestant work ethic.

It is admittedly also a factor that in the process the traditional criteria of being "pleasing" and of "artistic beauty" have also shifted. Or better, that within the context of today's art business various aesthetic parameters exist alongside each other. Certainly, quite a few present representatives of the architectural mainstream would like to join Hilmer & Sattler in invoking Kant's idealistic aesthetics. On the other hand, anyone who takes a lead from the artistic avant-garde (or, *grosso modo*, from the "romantic" tradition), will resist precisely this tradition. He (or she) will consider it more up-to-date and promising to use "bad" taste deliberately as an aesthetic weapon, on the one hand in order to "pick up" the "man in the street" on the plane of his visual habits, and on the other hand to appear "pleasing" to élites familiar with the strategies of irony and slapstick – in just the same way as Venturi does it with his frivolous mixture of historical architecture and fast food icons. Kant's contemporary Voltaire would perhaps have found Venturi's shrill American commercial burlesque on the theme of Cole's "Dream of an architect" tasteless – if not even the sign of a sick mind (as a *maladie de l'esprit*: "Depraved taste in art lies in taking pleasure in objects that disgust well-formed minds; preferring the burlesque to the noble, the precious and the affected to something that is beautiful purely and simply: that is a sickness of the mind."[30] And yet: it is precisely the "disturbed" aspect of this panorama that links unmistakably with an 18th century art form: the *capriccio*.

Hilmer & Sattler and Albrecht Architekten: Staatliche Gemäldegalerie in Berlin, 1986-1998. Interior view

The Reproducibility of Taste
Ákos Moravánszky

[1] translated by Michael Robinson; original German text: „Es ist keine Lage, wo Sinnlichkeit und Verstand, in einem Genusse vereinigt, so lange fortgesetzt und so oft mit Wohlgefallen wiederholt werden können, – als eine gute Mahlzeit in guter Gesellschaft. (…) Der ästhetische Geschmack des Wirts zeigt sich nun in der Geschicklichkeit, allgemeingültig zu wählen; welches er aber durch seinen eigenen Sinn nicht bewerkstelligen kann." Since different dishes please different palates, the host must invest in variety, so that „für jeden nach seinem Sinn einiges angetroffen werde; welches eine komparative Allgemeingültigkeit abgibt." Kant, Immanuel: Anthropologie in pragmatischer Hinsicht, ed. by Brandt, Reinhard (Hamburg: Felix Meiner Verlag, 2000) p. 157; full English text in: Kant, Immanuel: *Anthropology from a Pragmatic Point of View*, trans. Mary J. Gregor (The Hague, 1974)

[2] Ekuan, Kenji: *The Aesthetics of the Japanese Lunchbox* (Cambridge, Mass.: The MIT Press, 1998)

Bento: Japanese lunchbox

When Immanuel Kant bought himself a house in Königsberg in 1787, he offered his friends open house for lunch at any time. In the *Anthology from a Pragmatic Point of View*, the philosopher discusses the beautiful and the sublime, but also mentions hostly responsibilities: "There is no situation where sensuality and reason, enjoyed conjointly, can be so long continued and so often repeated with satisfaction – like a good meal in good company. (…) The aesthetic taste of the host is manifest here in the skill of making universally valid choices; but he cannot effect this through his own senses." Since different dishes please different palates, the host must invest in variety, so that "there is something for everyone according to his taste; which results in comparative general validity".[1] This comparative general validity requires careful choice; reason must accompany taste. While every guest is entitled to argue against another's opinion, they must all agree to the effect that they are enjoying a good meal and conducting an interesting conversation. A conversation where everyone agreed about everything would be boring, while an argument between two people who have nothing in common would merely degenerate into a cacophony of egoistic positions.

Perhaps this programme is realised pictorially in the *bento*, the Japanese lunchbox with its little sections containing tiny portions of roast, boiled and simmered, hot, sweet and sour dishes. The Japanese industrial designer Kenji Ekuan describes the bento as a mandala, a meditative image of the world, an encounter between produce of the sea and of the mountains, as a landscape that does not seem unregulated and picturesque like an English garden, but is arranged on a square grid pattern. The shape of the arrangement creates a connection between the various elements. It is strictly and hierarchically structured, but embodies a higher idea of an order imposed from without, and demands a free interpretation by the designer.[2]

So it is about filling the world with a wide range of visual stimuli: a car with a telephone, air conditioning, CD player, navigation system and drinks holders is ultimately following the aesthetic of the Japanese *bento* as an example of "comparative general validity," of universality manifested in diversity. Implementing this idea at the Königsberg lunch table within a progressive time scheme cannot have been easy and required a correspondingly long sequence of dishes.

The architecture of eating is the spatial and temporal organisation of the raw materials, it implies spaces and rituals and extends from planning to execution, from shopping at the market to serving the dessert. As the difference between Kant's meal and the *bento* shows, both architectural and gastronomic work can be understood only within a fabric of cultural conventions, theories, techniques and rituals. For centuries both architects and cooks strove to expound their perception of these connections in the forms of treatises, instructions or recipe collections. In both cases, this meant not only recording and retrospectively rationalising a creative process, but a concrete challenge to imitate it – with the promise that the imitator will be guided along new paths.

The invention of letterpress printing made it possible to take knowledge that had formerly been handed down through verbal explanations and above all by imitation in guilds and on building sites, or in the kitchen, and to marshal it within a system of clearly formulated principles, captured in writing and made accessible to a much wider public. In the 13th and 14th centuries records were still imprecise and scarcely organised. The recipes were more like aides-mémoire than instructions. In the course of time, this developed into today's flourishing production of about 20,000 new cookery books every year, often in print-runs of tens of thousands. They are compiled according to a variety of principles, for example by seasons, with their own seasonal ingredients and culinary languages, or sometimes going so far as to include suggestions for healthy eating.

It is not surprising that printed books led to comparable ordering and classifying processes for rules and experiences in all spheres of knowledge, intended to pass experiences on, and work out theoretical principles. It is a long way from the private recipe collection as a secret aide-mémoire, or from the construction drawing of a Gothic pinnacle kept by the masons' guild, to the emergence of a major book project like Sebastiano Serlio's *Nine Books about Architecture* (1537-1551) or Vignola's *Regola delli cinque ordini d'architettura* (1562). The idea that written instructions actually make it possible to prepare healthy, tasty dishes or create practical, beautiful buildings has always been (and will always be) questioned. In Serlio's eyes, even reducing the wealth of ancient architecture to five column orders was a compromise, so formulated that even moderately talented architects could achieve these ambitious ideals to some extent. But there was never any doubt that true masters do not need instructions like these.

The possibility of manual reproduction made the parallels between cookery books and architectural treatises more than a mere analogy, and this happened at the point where authors also started discussing the spatial context of cooking. Questions about home economics in general were now addressed alongside the systematisation of recipes, along with women's duties: their relationships with their husbands and the servants, the rooms in the house and how to arrange, clean and maintain them, and the health of their occupants. Here, for the woman, the home economics treatise becomes a kind of instruction manual for the house, that architect's product for which architectural treatises were written.

Let us consider the treatises that have discussed home life since ancient times rather more closely in connection with these home economics books. Xenophon's Oeconomicus was written in the 5th century, a work that required strict allocations to rooms in a house for men and women. Leon Battista Alberti's book *Della Famiglia* ("Domestic Life"), which bases itself on Xenophon's ideas, describes the house and its rooms as an instrument for disciplining the woman, who is moody by nature and has to be educated to accept order by men.[3] Marie Susanne Kübler's *Das Hauswesen nach seinem ganzen Umfange* ("The home in all its scope"), a cookery and home economics book that went into a number of new editions, also seems to follow this pattern. It is written in the form of letters to a female friend, and deals with subjects like order, cleanliness, frugality, but also the family table, the kitchen, the larder, dietary principles, nursing the sick etc. The young female readers are even warned, in the last letter about "training the mind," to avoid poems by poets who "unfortunately most often stray into the political, and thus create nothing truly poetic."[4]

Title page of Marie Susanne Kübler's book *Das Hauswesen nach seinem ganzen Umfange*

[3] Alberti, Leon Battista: *Über Hauswesen* (Stuttgart, Zurich: Artemis, 1962)

[4] Kübler, Marie Susanne: *Das Hauswesen nach seinem ganzen Umfange dargestellt in Briefen an eine Freundin mit Beigabe eines vollständigen Kochbuches* (Stuttgart: J. Engelhorn, 1867)

Raw materials

Systems relating to raw materials, rooms and rituals, which can be applied to architecture as well as to culinary or domestic subjects, indicate the consequences of drawing borders, establishing symmetries and asymmetries. Alberti's theses about the right basis for the household, intended to defined spatial contexts in family and state, home and city, are based on the concept of an economy the book examines right down to its sexual and symbolic implications. The anthropologist Claude Lévi-Strauss

[5] Lévi-Strauss, Claude: *The Raw and the Cooked* (Chicago: University of Chicago Press, 1983)

was the first person to conduct a systematic structural investigation avant la lettre in the 1960s, in the course of his research in the villages of the original inhabitants of Latin America. Lévi-Strauss analysed food and its raw materials analogously with the spoken language, as both products are elements of the same culture. He examined the form in which concepts like "symbol" and "metaphor" can be applied to the analysis of eating and architecture. Lévi-Strauss's works like *Le cru et le cuit* ("The Raw and the Cooked"; 1970) identify the rules controlling our everyday lives.[5] Raw materials, food preparation technologies, habits – all these are components of a system of signifiers. Communication takes place through eating to a significant extent.

[6] Douglas, Mary: *Purity and Danger. An Analysis of the Concepts of Pollution and Taboo* (London and New York: Routledge, 1966), p. 34

[7] Lévi-Strauss, Claude, op. cit.

From the outset, cookery books gave health advice as well, with instructions on diet and the healing effects of kitchen herbs. Here, consciously or subconsciously, they are taking on the various prohibitions of religious origin regulating handling raw materials and their suitability for consumption. The American anthropologist Mary Douglas described these prohibitions in her book *Purity and Danger*. She analyses the differences between cooked and raw food. For example, in Hindu India, fruit and nuts are considered pure only when intact. As soon as a coconut is broken open or a banana cut into, a Brahmin can no longer accept it from someone of a lower caste. Such commands are often explained in terms of hygiene. The Jewish and Islamic ban on eating pork, for example, is based on the dangers posed by rotten meat in hot areas.[6]

So distinction between food and poison seems to represent an unambiguous separation, hiding behind other boundary settings, e.g. of a religious nature. But in his structural anthropology, Lévi-Strauss shows that for the South American Nambikwara, who are very experienced poison-mixers, foodstuffs and poisons are not mutually exclusive categories.[7] According to this, the boundaries between raw material categories for food are just as fluid as those between building materials, despite assertions to the contrary by many architects about the identity of brick or of wood, for example, which formed the basis for many construction system manuals, and continues to do so.

[8] Semper, Gottfried: *Der Stil in den technischen und tektonischen Künsten oder praktische Aesthetik* (vol. 1 Frankfurt am Main: Verlag für Kunst und Wissenschaft, 1860; vol. 2 Munich: Friedrich Bruckmann, 1863).

[9] Forster, Kurt W.: *Schmelzkäse oder Fondue*, in Oswald, Franz, Schüller, Nicola (eds.): *Neue Urbanität. Das Verschmelzen von Stadt und Landschaft* (Zurich: gta Verlag, 2003), pp. 130-146

The architect and architectural theoretician Gottfried Semper established a system of materials for architecture in which symbolic links play an important part as well. He set up four categories for primal technologies corresponding with four characters of materials. *Textile art* is work with thin, elastic materials. The result is a two-dimensional textile, the material used for the first room divisions, the inside walls of a house. *Ceramics* works with soft, plastic masses that can be kneaded, and then hardened (e.g. fired or dried). *Tectonics* means fitting hard, bar-like elements together in a rigid system. Wood is the original tectonic material, while the tectonic objects are not firmly fastened to the ground. A roof truss is an important example of this. *Stereotomy*, finally, is work with heavy, hard materials that resist pressure well – in other words stone or brick. *Masonry*, cutting hard materials into smaller units and piling them on top of each other, is part of this.[8]

The most important feature of Semper's system is its flexibility: the boundaries of his four basic categories are permeable. One material can take on the role of another at any time. It is a matter of imitation, presentation and theatricality. A beautifully crafted brick wall can play the part of a textile covering. In just the same way, bowls pressed in plastic can imitate the form of crystal glass. In architecture as in gastronomy, the modern notion of appropriate materials has caught on. Post-war cookery books, with their false cream soups made of dried milk powder and cakes based on dried peas and flour, show that an emergency can lead to surrogates. This is the only possible excuse for individual ingredients without their own identity, consistency and structure. But under normal circumstances, fish should clearly not be meat. Unclearly defined consistencies like porridge, syrup and brawn often acquire negative connotations – just like the earlier attitudes to opaque glass in architecture. When discussing the way town and country are merging together in Switzerland in an essay, Kurt W. Forster drew an analogy with the creamy consistency of fondue.[9]

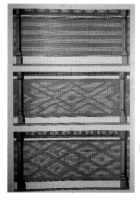

Decorative brick cladding in Pierre Chabat: *La brique et la terre cuite* 1920

Semper used the term *Stoffwechsel* (lit. material-swap; metabolism) to describe formal transfer in architecture, and the work is significant in the kitchen as well. The German word comes from chemistry: Justus Liebig, the inventor of meat extract, introduced it around 1840 to describe the transformation, the cycle of materials in nature. Semper was no longer interested in fixed identities, but in transformations. If a brick wall looks like a textile surface, it triggers cultural memory, a temporal connection with an earlier stage. In Semper's theory, *Stoffwechsel* almost moves towards greater durability in architecture: stone or metal take over the roles of shorter-lived materials like textiles or timber.

The thing that links metabolism in its culinary and architectural sense is political economics, as it were, creating added value. Alvar Aalto said this of Frank Lloyd Wright in his Vienna lecture *Between Humanism and Materialism*: "I was once in Milwaukee with my old friend Frank Lloyd Wright, who was giving a lecture there, and he started like this: 'Do you know what a brick is., ladies and gentlemen? It is a trifle, it costs 11 cents, it is a worthless, banal thing, but it has one particular quality. Give me this brick and it will immediately be transformed into the value of its weight in gold.' It was perhaps the only time I heard an audience told so brutally and vividly what architecture is. Architecture is turning a worthless brick into a golden brick."[10] In fact both architecture and culinary delicacies are created by value adding processes that can never be quite explained in terms of reason. It is not enough to know the rule, you need to make quick decisions based on taste and intuition. *On devient cuisinier, mais on naît rôtisseur* – "You become a cook, but you're born to roast," said Jean-Anthelme Brillat-Savarin, author of the *Physiology of Taste*.[11] *On devient ingénieur, mais on naît architecte*, countered the French architect Auguste Perret. The physiology of taste can be analysed down to the last detail, but masterpieces still resist reproduction.

[10] Aalto, Alvar: *Between Humanism and Materialsm*, (New York: Museum of Modern Art, 2002)

[11] Brillat-Savarin, Jean-Anthelme: *Physiologie des Geschmacks oder Transzendentalgastronomische Betrachtungen* (Leipzig: Philipp Reclam jun., n.y.), p. 24

[12] Kübler, *op.cit.*, p. 7

[13] Muche, Georg: "Das Versuchshaus des Bauhauses", in Adolf Meyer (ed.), *Ein Versuchshaus des Bauhauses in Weimar* (Munich: Albert Langen Verlag, 1923), pp. 15-16

[14] Frederick, Christine: *Household Engineering. Scientific Management in the Home* (Chicago: American School of Home Economics, 1920)

[15] Meyer, Erna: *Der neue Haushalt – Ein Wegweiser zu wirtschaftlicher Hausführung* (Stuttgart: Franck'sche Verlagshandlung, 1926)

[16] Taut, Bruno: *Die Neue Wohnung. Die Frau als Schöpferin* (3rd ed. Leipzig: Klinkhardt & Biermann, 1925), p. 99

Spaces

Order in deeds, order in space and order in time: these are the three commandments Marie Susanne Kübler derived from the "laws of an eternal order" and passed them on to the housewife. Human activity should "be regulated by a system of order," and a "spirit of order" should "lend a woman's work in the home a higher value, and order should be the track on which the little world in which the woman rules moves forward, silent and secure."[12] In Kübler's day this order in deeds, time and space meant above all supervising the maid, whose time and space was regulated to the last detail. Once women had to ensure order in space and time themselves, without any servants, and thus take on new tasks, the rationalisation of the kitchen speeded up. Georg Muche wrote about this in the Bauhaus Book *Ein Versuchshaus des Bauhauses in Weimar* ("An experimental house by the Weimar Bauhaus"), saying that the "wrong furnishing of the kitchen, often in terms of the room itself" was the root of problems "resulting in undue loss of time. The kitchen should be the housewife's work-place, her laboratory, in which every superfluous element of the room's size and every awkward arrangement of the furnishings constantly create extra work. The kitchen must become a mechanism, an instrument. Time should be too valuable for the woman of the house for her to tolerate the drudgery of old-fashioned kitchen management day in, day out."[13]

The much-used terms Taylorism and Fordism, from the field of industrial management, were applied directly in so-called domestic Taylorism. The American Christine Frederick, industrial advisor and pioneer of domestic ergonomics, analysed kitchen work between 1915 and 1922. In her famous experiments she tied a thread to her assistants' feet. It gradually unrolled, and Frederick was able to establish what distances the housewife covered in a day. The result was a network of lines running all over the room. Once the furniture was grouped in work zones the pattern became much simpler.[14] Her book was translated into German in 1921, followed five years later by Erna Meyer's guide *Der Neue Haushalt – Ein Wegweiser zu wirtschaftlicher Hausführung* ("The New Household – A pointer towards economical household management"). The author had devised the design principles for the kitchens in the Weißenhofsiedlung, leading most famously to Margarete Schütte-Lihotzky's Frankfurt Kitchen.[15] Bruno Taut also concurred with the results of Christine Frederick's studies in his new book *Die Neue Wohnung: Die*

Frau als Schöpferin ("The New Dwelling: the Woman as Creator";1924), but he saw the main purpose of the "redemption of the woman" as winning her round to the aims of *Neues Bauen*: "The man will now be able to build the house only when his path has been freed by the redemption of the woman. His freedom, mobility, and readiness for the path that is already in place, will be a consequence of the liberation of the woman; for every form of slavery also draws in that person who outwardly and apparently does not have to suffer under it."[16] Work in the kitchen was not just made easier, the new, initially fairly monstrous pieces of equipment soon became friendly aids, beautifully designed objects, and conversation pieces at dinner parties. Domestic mechanisation begins in the kitchen.

Illustration from Christine Frederick's book *Household Engineering*

Christine Frederick: *Household Engineering*

"Consider electric refrigerators and skyscrapers and bathroom equipment. This is where to look for the development of a genuine modernism!", wrote Egmont Arens in 1931 in an essay called *Imagination for sale* published in the magazine *Advertising Arts*.[17] The way into the new world of modern architecture is through the refrigerator door: you open it, and have the whole

[17] Arens, Egmont: *Imagination for Sale, Advertising Arts* (November 1931), pp.22-23

[18] Fitch, James Marston: *Architecture and the Esthetics of Plenty* (New York and London: Columbia University Press, 1961)

[19] Kennedy, Robert Woods: *The House and The Art of its Design* (New York: Reinhold Publishing Co., 1953), pp. 234-135

magnificent array of ham, cold cuts, cheese, creams and cakes before your eyes. Heaped mounds of oranges and sausages were already among the sights at the Chicago World Fair in 1893, and soon the American *Aesthetics of Plenty* was to become an architectural programme that needs large areas of glass, above all for presenting abundance.[18] New cookery books and collections of recipes were addressing the task of organising a wealth of new, exotic foods and domestic gadgets. One book that was particularly important as a handbook for housewives and at the same time as a programme for a modern kind of American architecture was *The House and the Art of its Design*, 1953, by Robert Woods Kennedy, an architect who worked in Gropius's and Breuer's practices and who was a close friend of the architect William Wurster. Kennedy's book warned against the dangers of rationalisation, and identified the importance of individual habits, but he also followed the ordering discipline of the domestic books by precisely defining and locating the various occasions and places for eating, for example, the participants, the equipment, crockery and cutlery needed and the way they should be stored.[19]

The increasing systematisation of the household and cooking as a result of such publications established the basis for the functional reorganisation of the home, from domestic mechanisation to preparing food and its ingredients industrially. But this systematisation is accompanied by attempts to escape. Despite the fact that takeaway sounds modern, people have always eaten away from hearth and home. The hiker's snack, the peasant's sparse meal, down to the standing menu in snack cafés – "takeaway" can take many forms, often associated with hard work, illness and the infirmity of old age. But then successful escape attempts like barbecuing in the garden show that we are still living in a refined system that also regulates these short, ritualised flights.

Agricultural exhibition at the 1893 exhibition in Chicago

Robert Woods Kennedy: *The House and the Art of its Design* (title page)

Frankfurt Kitchen on the Römerstadt housing estate, type A, 1926

"Among the many delights in life that human acuity can place before us, a good meal will commonly top the list, especially for the men. You would not believe, my dear Frida, how such a thing can influence the mood of a man, and so you will do well if when faced with the weakness – no, I don't want to call it that, for just as the eye delights in the beautiful, the ear in melodies and the sense of smell in fragrances, so the palate may revel in that which tastes pleasing – you will do well if you consider this inclination duly" – warned Marie Susanne Kübler.[20] Eating as a physiological function and eating as a form of social behaviour are the two extremes used by authors of books on cooking, household management and architecture. Robert Woods Kennedy emphasises the "ritualistic importance" of eating: "The food eaten, the way in which the table is set, the family's manners are all highly potent symbols of class status. 'Nice' people have 'refined' table manners. The family feels that the guest will necessarily watch for the little indications of culture and refinement, while the guest feels embarrassed to have unwittingly invaded the family's privacy. Thus dining spaces located where they can be viewed from the entrance are anathema for most people. They should be as private as the family feels; their atmosphere should suggest the degree of ritual which the family enjoys; and their appointments should be the most elegant."[21]

The "class" Kennedy is invoking is of course no longer defined by birth, but by social success, which can also be read from table manners. The reform culture at the turn of century, which placed the "natural human being" at the centre, addressed the cult of the body left as nature intended, but also the control of the body and body language as a necessity of civilisation. Modernism's how-to-behave books like for example Berta Wittstock's *Was ist richtig? Was ist falsch? Warum?* ("What is right? What is wrong? Why?") also concentrate on eating as a natural yet culturally shaped process, but with aesthetic insights and not prohibitions as orientation points: "The aesthete makes no use of the knife at all for dishes containing no meat, and he is quite right to do so."[22]

Roland Barthes, the French cultural philosopher, who studied everyday signs and their cultural meanings, constructed "his" Japan as a counter to the martial European world of eating with a knife and fork. In his book "Empire of Signs," Japanese eating rituals are thus presented as diametrically opposed to European ones. For him, eating with chopsticks is not a mechanical operation, but spatial calligraphy: the chopsticks show, select, pick up the little morsels with very little pressure.[23] The present vogue for eating sushi shows how ideas are shifting from hot to cold in terms of spatial aesthetics and the thermal symbolism of eating as well.

Illustration from Berta Wittock

Gropius House, Lincoln Massachusetts, designed together with Marcel Breuer 1937-1938

Robert Woods Kennedy also stressed the thermal importance of the kitchen in 1953: "Here is heat, fire, steam, smells, usually wonderful but sometimes awful, and a mysterious chemical process which, because it is superintended by a woman, makes her into a sort of genie. Here is the female symbol of creative heat, which she can only regard with the greatest of awe – even as her husband regards his fireplace."[24]

[20] Kübler, *op.cit.*, p. 43

[21] Ibid, p. 239

[22] Wittstock, Berta: *Was ist richtig? Was ist falsch? Warum? Gesellschaftliche Umgangsformen der Gegenwart* (Berlin: Die Brücke, 1931), p. 47

[23] Barthes, Roland: *Empire of signs* (Hill and Wang, 1986)

[24] Kennedy, *op. cit*

In the meantime, the kitchen has become colder both thermally and aesthetically, but it has gained space. With its high-quality built-in equipment and designer objects like Philip Starck's *Juicy Salif* lemon squeezer or Ron Arard's *Chiringuito* cocktail shaker, it provides a background for conversation and somewhere to put the cookery book collection. Picture books offering an atmospheric presentation of landscapes, buildings and recipes are popular. But the mere act of flicking through them offers synaesthetic delight, a journey through India, Thailand or Japan on the sofa.

Like architecture books, the new cookery books owe their popularity to personalities whose auras stand for the quality of the works presented in the age of their mechanical reproducibility. These personalities used to be so-called master-chefs, now the life and work of well-known artists like Paul Gauguin, Claude Monet or Frida Kahlo serve as a narrative framework and pictorial background for gastronomic presentations. The more the flavour of standardised tomatoes and peppers from Dutch greenhouses dwindles, the more colourful the pictures get. Here it does not matter whether the recipes are taken over in slightly modified form from older, less attractively designed collections. No one cooks them anyway. Where would you find 1 kg of Romeritos, six Nopales cut into strips, 14 Guajillo chillies and two Ancho chillies to cook your guests a *Revoltillo*?[25] Paradoxically, it is precisely the exotic-sounding names of these unfamiliar and unobtainable ingredients that contribute to the "Mexican atmosphere" that made you buy the book in the first place. The fact that the dishes presented cannot be reproduced is essential if the aura of the image as a food surrogate is to be created. *The pictorial turn*, a concept the art theoretician W.J.T. Mitchell coined to define the fundamental cultural change of our times, is taking place in all spheres of life. So we will have to wait even longer for Salvador Dalí's prophecy to be fulfilled: in an essay for the Surrealist magazine *Minotaure* he described the structural elements of Gaudí's Sagrada Familia cathedral as consisting of tender calf's liver, and then declared his cannibalistic appetite for art: *La beauté sera comestible ou ne sera pas* ("Beauty must become edible, or it must disappear").[26] As this and other publications prove, it is in fact the beauty of the image that triumphs over the other senses.

[25] Rivera, Guadalupe; Colle, Marie-Pierre: *Frida's Fiestas. Recipes and Reminiscences of Life with Frida Kahlo* (New York: Clarkson Potter, 1994)

[26] Dalí, Salvador: "De la beauté terrifiante et comestible de l'architecture modern style", in *Minotaure* no. 3-4 (December 1933), pp. 69-76

1950s picnic basket

Meaningful Architecture in a Globalised World
Gion Caminada

Telephone box, 1997

When I'm designing, I'm at the same time exercised by the problems of this world. With my architecture I try to help solve these problems. For me, building is a way of life. I have built little things, a telephone box, a mortuary, at the moment I am designing a public toilet, and above all, houses, all sorts of things that people need for their lives. Beauty is not the first consideration. I cannot persuade a farmer that he should build a beautiful cowshed. But if the cowshed works well, then it can be beautiful too. In other words, architecture must meet a need. I do not explain my buildings in terms of complicated theoretical edifices or arbitrary artistic inspirations. That is not quite enough for me. In fact, I believe that architecture, which always derives from an idea, embraces a totality of events in which a kind of sensuality can be discerned. I build to endow a real need with built form. I was recently talking to a curator of historic monuments about a new building regulation. He said that the regulation must lay down that building has to meet a certain minimum standard. But how is quality "as such" to be built? Architecture has first of all to fulfil a function, be meaningful in some way. This comes before quality. That has always been the case. If a building makes sense, quality comes into being. It determines quality. A good design embodies a totality of all events and also has the capacity to tell stories. Something has to come into being that was not determined in advance. I want there to be stories, and so I build houses for eternity.

Mountain village of Vrin, the Grisons

83

Mortuary in Vrin, 2002. Placed symbolically, physically and atmospherically between the everyday world of the village and the religious precinct with cemetery and church: also reflected in the white-painted wood

Staircase in the mortuary

Details of the corner joints

Let us look at the mortuary I built in Vrin. What was needed here was to find a way of dealing with death. Death is really always present in life. The media constantly report on events relating to death. And yet it is a typical feature of our society that it suppresses death. The "stiva da morts" addresses this suppression. And it concretises the theme of mourning. The dead cannot mourn. So the mortuary is visibly outside the Vrin cemetery in the secular area – at the point where the boundary between life and death runs for many people. Mourning is ambivalent, and always involves both laughing and crying, or exulting in life. I talked to the people of Vrin for a long time about what it means to mourn. I had to be provocative to make sure that something would emerge. The Vriners were not particularly bothered about the location of the mortuary. But they did feel provoked when I asked them if they could imagine drinking coffee in the mortuary. People used to tell jokes during the laying out. This did little harm to the dead person, but it helped the living to get over the death. The division into three spaces, with the mortuary room, kitchen and corridor – a typical house typology – creates a secular place for domestic mourning for the dead. The Vriners take pride in their mortuary now, because it works. They allowed themselves to be seduced by the architectural idea.

Something that concerns me very much in the present day is the levelling caused by the time-space-differences. In our globalised world our living space is becoming increasingly smaller. How can we make it bigger? I think we can do that by attempting to resist utterly uniform thinking, the levelling of values and the destruction of diversity. In our world, it is almost impossible for people to have fundamentally new experiences. I am working on a project called "The picture behind the picture" with my students at the ETH in Zurich. In contrast with the study being undertaken at the ETH in Basel with Roger Diener, Jacques Herzog, Pierre de Meuron, Marcel Meili and Christian Schmid we are not looking down at Switzerland as if at a map, which ultimately is the same as destroying diversity, we are looking at it from the inside. What can be activated from the inside, what resources are available? How can unspoilt areas like Bergell for example be given a chance? The forces coming from the inside are strong. It is no good simply prescribing from above how they should move. Our approach is to strengthen the periphery. Identity has become a key concept in the current planning culture debate. Identity is a matter of internal structures and differences. That is to say, the differences and also the boundaries between urban qualities and the periphery have to be clearly drawn. At the same time, better links are needed between the centre and the periphery. And if we are aiming to have a diverse country that can hold its own in the international competition between locations, it means having a better understanding of the images we carry within us of a house in Appenzell or Bergell. In these different places, whether it be Vrin or Appenzell villages, certain building traditions have developed over the centuries, and it is these traditions that have created the images. But the image we see is perhaps not the primary one. There is no such thing a *the* Appenzell house. But what has generated the image we have of it, where did it come from, what criteria, what qualities were important to make it emerge as it has? If we learn to understand these images behind the images, then we also find out how to think about developing the building tradition. Then it is possible to create diversity and new things within the tradition, without coming up with picturesque, superficial reproductions. People are longing for this diversity. And cooking is also about working against this levelling of taste. How many different, delicious, regional recipes there are!

86

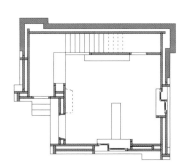  

Mortuary, ground plans and sections

Mortuary in Vrin

Girls' boarding school, "Lower House," part of the Disentis monastery, 2004

At the moment, I am building a house on a hill in the Appenzell countryside. The story of how it came into being explains my thinking: originally, there was already an architect drawing up plans. He wanted to build a house clad in aluminium on this site. But according to the building regulations, wood had to be used here. The local council did not want to give him planning permission. But the administrative court decided in his favour, as the architect intended to finish the aluminium cladding with wood paint. This made it into a wooden building. But that means: this architect has an image of an Appenzell house in mind. He is not interested in its typology and how it has changed over time. He wanted to rescue the image of the Appenzell house and take it forward – and he didn't care how he did it. My approach is different: I am interested in what the essential features of an Appenzell house are, what the basic idea behind it is. I have tried to integrate a new form for life within the usual way it is constructed. How can today's way of life be reconciled with the Appenzell typology? I think typology is the opposite of the model; a model can't be changed, otherwise it isn't one any longer. But a typology, which takes up information from all sorts of life habits, construction methods, geometries etc. is open to change. It is easy to identify which are the core elements that cannot be changed. Typology is as imprecise as a traditional recipe. It is the differences, the finer points that move, seduce, taste delicious. For example, repetition is something fantastic for me. If you look at a flock of sheep moving across the high Greina plain, 200 of them, side by side under the scudding clouds: there is nothing more moving. I find our modern cities extremely boring because of their visual diversity – and I am not contradicting myself by calling for regional diversity. The great charm of the old Italian cities lies in the varied repetition of basic typological patterns.

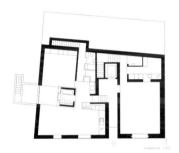  

Ground plans

Window detail in the girls' boarding school

Interior concrete core with stairs and corners for communal use

90

Segmüller House, Vignon, 2002

I think of a construction pretty quickly when I am designing. You don't just need the ingredients, you also need to know how to mix them, and the equipment you need to do that. Thinking about construction inevitably takes you to material. When construction and material are included early in the design process, then they both influence the idea of space. I am very interested in the interplay between cladding and construction. Where does one begin, and where does the other end? Here I am particularly interested in traditional *Strickbau* (literally "knitted construction"). This layering of timbers one on top of the other works best with compact cells. For this reason, cells used to be lined up next to each other. The traditional *Strickbau* house always has a combination of kitchen and a small living room, the kitchen being the key feature. The question arose for me of how the *Strickbau* house type could be re-used and adapted to the needs of modern life. First of all I made the corridors a little wider. Then I hit upon another design method. I started to place room cells in position and surrounded them with walls. In other words, I worked with spaces while I was designing, not with walls. Ultimately this made me realise that the construction can be very highly modulated when using this method, and it is not necessary to think exclusively in horizontals and verticals. So I cut more and more out of the body of the building, hollowed it out, as it were. This generated new, exciting spatial experiences. For my most recent *Strickbau*, I have investigated the principle of mass. No other timber construction has such a dense mass as *Strickbau*. That shows in the outward appearance of the mortuary. It is as though the wooden building is just as massively built as the stone church.

Traditional *Strickbau*

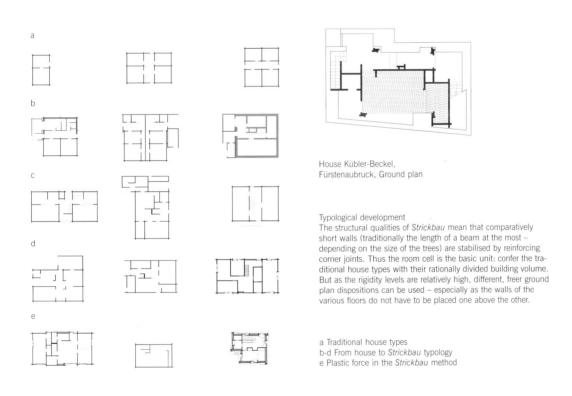

a

b

c

d

e

House Kübler-Beckel,
Fürstenaubruck, Ground plan

Typological development
The structural qualities of *Strickbau* mean that comparatively short walls (traditionally the length of a beam at the most – depending on the size of the trees) are stabilised by reinforcing corner joints. Thus the room cell is the basic unit: confer the traditional house types with their rationally divided building volume. But as the rigidity levels are relatively high, different, freer ground plan dispositions can be used – especially as the walls of the various floors do not have to be placed one above the other.

a Traditional house types
b-d From house to *Strickbau* typology
e Plastic force in the *Strickbau* method

91

If strengthening the periphery is to be deliberately lived out and promoted, then it also involves meaningful support for local craft and processing industries, i.e. maintaining jobs and craft skills. I used fir wood as a building material for the mortuary and many other buildings in and around Vrin. It is a material that could be felled, cut to size and processed on the spot. This renewable raw material costs next to nothing. But processing it can be a little more expensive. I could have chosen a "better" wood, like for example larch. But then the added value would not have been so great. And it is precisely this added value, deriving from low material costs, that I am concerned with. Value is added because of the special nature of the treatment. The same is true of cooking, when you cook something tasty with ingredients prepared on the spot, instead of opening a ready meal in a well-travelled tin. The strategy of enhancing a reasonably priced native material through a high degree of processing presents a meaningful challenge in terms of planning and craftsmanship for the builders as well. That is how building culture is created.

92

93

Building ensemble Sut Vitg situated just underneath the village of Vrin, 1998. The three new communal buildings (one is a slaughterhouse, the other two are barns) are part of the concept of strengthening the periphery by strengthening the local economy. For the slaughterhouse (on the right) Caminada developed a particularly refined *Strick* (knitting).

The Eater and his Ancestors
Andreas Hartmann

A woman remembers a weekly family ritual about preparing an apple pancake that was always served on Tuesdays when she was a child. The grandparents came to look after the little girl: "My grandma used to stand in the kitchen and stir the batter, in a big yellow stoneware bowl. While she was doing this my grandpa sat at the kitchen table with me, told stories and cut slices of apple, one for me – one for the pancake. The slices were cut off round the apple so that at the end a precisely cut cube was left round the core, and I gnawed this off as well. I can clearly remember those straight surfaces on the apple core that I bit into and left the pattern of my teeth. Then the apple slices were put in the batter while it was still wet, and it got drier and firmer and drew the apple slices into it, octagonal, hexagonal, square and almost round apple slices that floated on the batter like patches. When my grandma couldn't come any more my grandpa made the pancakes on his own. And later, when my grandpa was dead as well, my father took over making the apple pancakes. It is quite clear to me that the apples have to be cut just like my grandpa did for apple pancake. And I think that when my children start asking me about my grandparents the first thing I will tell them about them is this picture of Tuesday and the right way to make apple pancakes."

When we eat, our ancestors sit at the table with us. They are not just still present in family rituals, they are with us in the tastes and smells as well. Another woman tells us about the way taste and smell come together to form an unshakeable certainty about existence and origins in a little story about potatoes: "Onions, eggs, sausage and herbs were already finely chopped and diced in the bowl when I asked my grandmother to give me a potato that she had just peeled… She picked up the kitchen knife, cut a piece off the potato, carved a tiny sliver of butter off the edge of the piece of butter, dipped this in the salt cellar and spread both on the potato. Then, balancing the melting butter on top, she pushed the whole lot into my mouth with her hand. The smell of her hands mingled with the taste of the potato – each time she fed me a bit more I inhaled the fragrance first and only started to chew then, this good taste had all the best things in it that the world had ready for me. The mixture of smell, taste and situation triggered an incomparable feeling of safety and warmth. From that time, until my grandmother died – though I was 22 by then – I let her feed me this combination on potato salad days; and that feeling was always there…"

Our ancestors sit inconspicuously at the table with us, like a distant echo with every morsel. What we taste and what we like tasting is always partly the result of internalising cultural pre-programming as well, with the assistance of culinary education rituals at the family table. And the things that we assimilated when we were children will stay with us throughout our lives and whether we like it or not we will pass them on to the next generation in a more or less modified form. This was also the case for our parents, they were once children themselves, sitting at our grandparents' dining tables, who had themselves been socialised into a culinary world picture by their own parents. And so on. It would not be correct to imagine this handing-down process as a rigid transfer. On the contrary, it is a highly flexible communication process, open to all kinds of innovations and re-assessments; though certainly not to everything, and not at random, but always as part of deep-seated cultural pattern that cannot simply be abandoned at will. And the fact that our ancestors' authority persists despite all the changes in the culinary universe and general taste preferences shows for example in foods that are avoided with revulsion like rats, insects or dogs, which have persisted and remained stable in our cultural sphere over many generations.

Ancestors are frequently also present at celebratory meals, here in the form of shared memories. In cases where group memory, i.e. communicated memory is active, the ancestral line can admittedly not be too long. Communal memory illuminates a time-span of about 80 to 100 years in the direct exchange of experiences and stories, the memory limit is the biblical century. Children might possibly just hear conversation about their great-grandparents or even their great-great-grandparents at the family dining table, beyond that contemporary witnesses disappear and we finally end up on the territory of family legend and genealogy.

Nevertheless, celebratory meals in particular do provide a framework for collective memory and collective remembrance. It is not only in speeches at the table that we regularly come across a passage including those present symbolically, those who are physically present and those who are absent at this time, the deceased. Conversations at the table as well often circle around past feasts and meals eaten together in the distant past. They bring back to life times when the old people were still alive. People always like talking passionately about another meal at meals, and above all about the people who were there at the time. But it is not just about speeches and telling stories: there are also the memories that have accumulated around objects like a patina, a silver napkin ring perhaps, a wooden spoon that has worn smooth, an old-fashioned wineglass or item of cutlery, etc. These too are communication and ascertainment media, and can guarantee that the absent and the deceased will be virtually present in the communicative memory of the company at table. This group memory can acquire a three-dimensional quality through vivid demonstration: the mementoes might be linked with stories that then draw other stories in their wake, until finally a living visual memory emerges, literally bringing the remembered person so close as to be in touching distance – a vital manifestation, a collective narrative birth, a narrative reincarnation.

Food and drink, taste and smell are predestined in a particular way to stimulate memory. This is firstly linked with the fact that eating and drinking are social and communicative acts in their very essence, that to a certain extent all those people come together at every meal who have contributed to endowing taking nourishment with the wealth of meaning that goes beyond the mere function of absorbing calories. But it is also connected with the fact that the senses of smell and taste send their signals directly to the area of the brain that is responsible for generating emotions. And it is indeed striking that the memories represented in the culinary act are almost without exception emotionally charged and carry a powerful atmospheric content. The people we summon to the scene with the aid of culinary carrier media scarcely ever appear in our memories as neutral beings. And the rooms, the apartments and houses, the kitchens, cellars and storerooms, the gardens, street-corners, bakers' shops, classrooms or whatever locations they may be we associate with a certain characteristic smell or taste are not at all neutral either. They too carry an aura of familiarity, of a lost paradise or past fear, they too are bathed in an unmistakable light that means something fundamentally different from mere illumination. A spoonful of rice pudding, flavoured in a particular way, for example, is enough to make an elderly woman, able to collect the long-dead and fervently loved friends of her youth about her again in the festive and friendly glow of a childhood home decorated for Christmas, and to shake off the loneliness of old age.

So the luminous power of memory can reach a magnitude at which time seems to have been practically extinguished. Then we go on a journey through time, return to the feelings of our own body as a child, go back to the beginning. We experience the past as the present, and at the same time the people of yesteryear are re-presented today in sensual reality, present with us again. They do not simply dance before our eyes as images, they really are there, physically present. Their presence seems to be real, rather than a memory. A distinction can be made here between two ways of bringing this effect about. The first is the so-called *mémoire involontaire*, involuntary memory, which brings the past into the present unintentionally and invasively, as it were. Then we have *mémoire volontaire*, which induces these journeys in time with the aid of a carefully elaborated ritual programme.

In the private sphere, this could possibly develop in the form of the following two examples: "I am female, born in 1922. If I eat a dry roll and drink cold milk or cocoa with it – out of a white enamel mug – I think of the Maakendamm bathing beach by the Köhlbrand, date: 1932/33 … I have bought a white enamel mug specially. Then when I have a roll I wallow in memories of my holidays on the Maakendamm." And from the period immediately after the war: "… I was pulling a wooden cart behind me and hoping I'd meet a soldier at the fence who would give me his washing to do. It was a black GI. He gave me his uniform, his vests and his underpants, and wrote his name down for me. I can still remember: he was called Abraham.

I brought it all back the next day. My mother had washed the things by hand and ironed them beautifully. There really was chewing gum, and there was chocolate, and there were cigarettes and a tin of liver sausage. Never in my life – that's what I thought – had I eaten anything so good. It was like being in a land flowing with milk and honey. I was so happy! So if I'm in a bad mood today I go to the butcher and buy myself a quarter of liver sausage and eat it, and then I feel like I did then, and then I'm alright again."

Once more: the fascination of the culinary time machine lies in the real presence of the past, in the feeling of its coming back, really and genuinely. This return is represented as a direct sensual experience, as a physical feeling. Linked with this is an element of that strange self-enchantment that makes times that are chronologically separate merge into each other, against all mathematical and physical knowledge, a phenomenon that evades the explanatory premises of everyday reason. In that the past enters the consciousness in the form of real sentient, flesh-and-blood bodies in this way, at the same time it makes itself into a living memento about the structure of the world. Let us leave it open whether there is a universal effect behind this scheme that is innate in human nature; but perhaps one can speak carefully of a general disposition, an anthropologically given framework of possibility that permits the sensually real importation of the past into the present with the aid of culinary experiences. Now this framework of possibility finds an abundance of culture-specific forms in which quite different ideas of belief can be articulated, though this cannot alter the fact that these forms go beyond cultural and religious boundaries and relate food, rite and memory to each other, thus renewing man's cosmological order and relationship with the world through rites of return.

Let us therefore briefly address two complexes of rituals that are related to each other structurally but culturally quite far apart. In both, the category of the ancestor – in the sense of a relationship via descent – is conceptualised as food. First some remarks about the Last Supper. This rite is at the centre of Christian religious practice, it is at the same time the act of establishing the Church, certainty of salvation and the mystery of faith. I shall not go any more deeply into the so-called communion controversy about the conduct of the rite and the significance of its individual elements. But I will say this: the liturgical and exegetic coding of this key ritual is obviously not to be abandoned without dramatic consequences, indeed the very slightest change can potentially make the whole certainty of faith questionable. This seems to be the reason why the ecumenical compromise seems to be so difficult to achieve. And in fact the function of rituals is not in the first place to be flexible, but to secure the persistence of cultural and cosmological identity, to carry the stock of spiritual tradition through the ages and constantly regenerate it. Of course rituals change, but change is not their core message, rather, it is continuity, connections with descent.

The communion rite conceptualises this genealogical, community-forming connection as an assignment for the future and promise of redemption. Certainly the different variants of its celebration operate with the categories of food, the ritual meal, of memory and of transfer to the present, but there is dissent about the question of how these categories should be brought into play in each case: whether we – as for the Reformed Churches – should see the bread and wine as symbols of Christ's body or – as for the Lutherans and Catholics – as the Redeemer's physical presence; in what way – in the latter case – the mystery of the transformation takes place, and whether it must be a consecrated priest and thus a spiritual descendant of the Apostles who is permitted to speak the words of establishment; whether the body is to be passed over in one or two forms; whether the Eucharist is just a celebration of memory and communal thanks or over and above this a rite of sacrifice and act of redemption.

Some Biblical passages: "And as they were eating," it says in Mark's gospel, "he took bread, and blessed, and broke it, and gave it to them, and said: Take, this is my body. And he took a cup, and when he had given thanks he gave it to them, and they all drank of it. And he said to them: This is my blood of the covenant, which is poured out for many." And according to Luke and Paul, Jesus also said: "Do this in remembrance of me," and Paul additionally quotes the Saviour as saying: "For as often as you eat this bread and drink the cup, you proclaim the Lord's death until he comes." The cannibalistic scandal contained in the words of the establishment of the sacrament is openly put into words in John's account of the wondrous feeding: "I am the living bread which came down from heaven; if any one eats of this bread he will live for ever; and the bread which I shall give for the life of the world is my flesh." The Jews then disputed among themselves, saying: 'How can this man give us his flesh to eat?' So Jesus said to them, 'Truly, truly I say to you, unless you eat the flesh of the Son of man and drink his blood, you have no life in you; he who eats my flesh and drinks my blood has eternal life, and I will raise him up at the last day. For my flesh is food indeed, and my blood is drink indeed. He who eats my flesh and drinks my blood abides in me and I in him.' Many of his disciples, when they heard it, said, 'This is a hard saying; who can listen to it?'"

Understanding the Last Supper on the basis of the mystery of transubstantiation carries the above-mentioned phenomenon of

Giotto di Bondone: The Last Supper, 1305

the real presence into the material quality of the food itself. The memory awoken in the ritual meal is at the same time an astonishing form of representation, a directly corporeal restoration of the crucified Christ to the present. This representation perceives itself as a gift, linking the first founder of the Church with his present congregation uninterruptedly over the centuries, and at the same time connecting God's creation work desecrated by man into the redemption of the world. In this respect the communion gift is an essential component of an exchange system that aims at restoring cosmological order, at the coming of the Kingdom of God and the completion of the circle of history.

In the encyclical Ecclesia de Eucharistia dating April 17, 2003, John Paul II identified this dynamic of gift and counter-gift with almost ethnological precision. "This," he writes, "is the *mysterium fidei*, that becomes present in the Eucharist: the world, that came out of the hands of the creator God returns to God as the world redeemed by Christ." This telos is fulfilled through the sacrifice of the Son of man, which was a gift to the Father in its turn, a gift that he returned in the form of eternal life through the resurrection. By making this gift an eternal presence in the Eucharist, Jesus Christ established "a mysterious 'simultaneity' between that (first) triduum of the Easter mystery and the passing of all centuries."

To avoid misunderstandings: I am not trying to consider theological questions here, but to assess ethnologically the structural link between ritual meal, representation of the past and cosmology. In the case of the Last Supper we see that this link arises from a constellation of exchanged gifts that assists the cosmological determination of historical fulfillment and thus also creates socio-religious guide values, perhaps to the extent that the Church perceives itself as a body in its turn, giving itself up to God in heaven. It hardly needs to be particularly emphasised that the ritual complex of the Eucharist is also directly bound up with architectural programmes, as the first communion room represents the prototype of all eucharistic mnemotopes that we fundamentally have to address as altar and church structures. The papal encyclical insists on this emphatically.

The second example takes us to North-East Thailand, to a hut village not far from the Cambodian border. Here, I was able to record a ritual that also creates an association between feeding, memory and cosmology, though in a different way. Memory happens here in the actual literal sense of "in-gesting." The whole of North-East Thailand is dominated by a marked belief in spirits, and in this special ritual women invite those ancestors to visit who lived in prehistoric mythical times, as bringers of culture. The outstanding cultural techniques that women have learned from these ancestors in an unbroken genealogical transmission include the whole art of weaving: breeding silkworms, reeling the silk, making the dye and the ikat dyeing process, knowledge about weaving patterns, etc. The ritual itself is an ecstasy ritual in the course of which the ancestors physically enter the women's bodies. Then the women, transformed into their own ancestors and dressed in silk, dance around a pedestal in a ceremonial place into the small hours. Everyone helps to prepare the feast. Children, young people, men, women. A ceremonial ladder is leaned against the pedestal in the middle of the ceremonial square, and the ancestors climb down this at

Thai ritual: association of feeding, memory and cosmology

the beginning of the ritual. Sacrificial gifts are draped, foodstuffs prepared. A kind of navigation light shows the ancestors the way. This is where the food offerings are placed later. The kitchen fire also burns all the time, and here chicken, soup and other things are prepared. Cords decorated with flowers, fruit and sweetmeats span the square. In the course of the night the incarnated ancestors "shoot" the fruit with the aid of ceremonial weapons, thus reliving the invention of hunting, agriculture and trade.

Music starts at the beginning of the actual trance ritual. The ancestors are then invoked and served with food. Via the pedestal and the ceremonial ladder they enter water-drawing containers, decorated with flowers and candles according to strict rules. From there they enter the women's bodies, often causing convulsions like epilepsy. The women grasp the water-drawing vessels in their hands and incarnate themselves in them. Now they take on the identity of their ancestress, and deck themselves in silk. A twelve-year old girl who is being initiated, whose ecstasy I was also able to capture on video, changed her whole manner and bearing throughout the entire ritual. Her ancestress Dschampi (a flower name) now dwelt in her mortal body. The other participants also recognised the ancestress's real return in the form of this twelve-year-old in the course of this "visit," and joyfully welcomed an 84-year-old, highly venerated mistress who had lived many thousands of years ago. The girl/Dschampi also danced all night with the other women. The dance continued into the morning hours, embedded in various ritual chores, one of which was feeding the ancestors.

The understanding of the ritual participants was that it was not the present-day women who were eating the ritual meal, but their progenitors, who left their bodies again the next day to return to their homes. The food must be right, the promise of offerings must be correctly fulfilled if the ancestress is to visit in order to secure genealogical continuity for another year, and with this the order of things. Here too – as in the private sphere sketched out above and in the ritual complex of communion in a quite different perspective – past and present mingle, here too the ritual meal is the agent; here too a kind of contract comes into play, and it is about no less that the structure of the world and the persistence of culture and of history: a history in which the simultaneity of beginning and end is also implicit. The eater and his ancestors, in the wider, socio-religious and ritual context, are bound up in cosmological orders – and everything suggests that the culinary cosmology of Modernism also operates with traditional attachments.

Thai ritual: sacrificial foods

Hearth and Home
Food Preparation Locations in Changing Times
Peter Davey

[1] Vitruvius: *De Architectura*, Book II, chapter I. Marcus Vitruvius Pollio's book is the only treatise on architecture to survive from Classical times.

It all began with fire. Vitruvius thought that we owe language itself, and hence civilisation, to fire[1]. Certainly, no human culture in any climate has been able to do without it completely; it has formed the basis for heating, defence, lighting, and of course for cooking and food preservation. No wonder that one of the most revered shrines in the Roman Forum was the Temple of Vesta, a circular stone abstraction of a primitive hut focussed on a central fire tended by six aristocratic virgins. If the fire were to go out, calamity would befall the state, just as it would any family living in a wattle and daub tepee in the forest.

In most cultures, fire continued to be the centre of social and familial life and the focus of the dwelling. From Viking huts in the north, where ingenious underfloor ducts were constructed from stone slabs to bring outside air to the central hearth without chilling the room, to the trulli, the beehive-shaped stone huts of Puglia in southern Italy, the central fire was the source of food, light, warmth and companionship. In the cities of the Roman Empire and the Middle East, a much more complex pattern of

[2] Similar devices, fuelled by specially made cylindrical cakes of compressed charcoal perforated to assist draft, are still in extensive use in China today.

food preparation emerged. In Pompeii and similar cities, the poor lived in insulae, dense multi-storey blocks of flats in which individual dwellings had no kitchens. Their inhabitants probably cooked at home (if they did so at all) on small portable charcoal-fuelled stoves,[2] which also served to heat the room. Bread came from the baker, whose oven was heated by lighting a fire inside it and raking out the embers when the oven itself was baking hot; almost certainly people would bring their own food: pies, pasties and roasts to cook in the baker's oven, as they did in many European countries well into the 20th century. The poor must also have patronised the many fast-food shops located on the ground floors of the insulae – here food was cooked and maintained hot in large bowls let into stone counters that faced the street: meals could be eaten on the premises or taken upstairs.

Pompeii: Street cookshop; cooking equipment was fitted into the round openings

For the rich, life was very different. Slaves prepared the food, and domestic stoves were common. They were masonry or clay platforms on which charcoal or wood was burned in a lattice of small interconnected chambers. Pots were heated in holes in the platform or on top of it, as they were in the fast-food shops. In many cases, stoves were in special rooms – the domestic kitchen was emerging, and from the first it was associated with wealth and privilege. Few seem to have worried much about what kitchens were like, for though slaves may have been rather more valuable than kitchen stoves, as personal possessions of their masters, they received no more empathy from most of their owners than an inanimate heap of bricks. Vitruvius gives virtually no advice about how to organise and position kitchens, though he goes into some detail about the proportions and orientation of dining rooms.[3]

In masonry houses, it was natural that the stove should be set against a wall, so the fire migrated from the centre of the room to its edge. Chimneys were evolved, according to some, in northern Italy in the 13th century.[4] Previously, smoke had been allowed to rise to be dispersed from the loft. Initially, chimneys were of wood, wattle and daub or wicker, formed into hoods over the fireplace – obviously prone to accidental fire, so where materials were available and owners were rich enough, chimneys were made of stone, and later brick. Chimneys had many advantages as well as the obvious one of getting rid of smoke. They were gradually developed to provide different forms of space-heating as well as means of cooking. In more elaborate versions, the strength of the fire could be moderated by baffles in the flue, and many forms of the stove evolved in Central and Northern Europe. In north China and Central Asia, sleeping platforms, heated on the hypocaust system, were formed next to the stove.

In cold, temperate and Mediterranean climates, the massive hearth and chimney structure acted as a heat store. Benches were often provided on both sides of the main fire of the house to form an inglenook, a cave-like place to which the family retired in the coldest times. In summer, chimneys provided a measure of ventilation. Meat and fish were preserved by being hung in the chimney to be smoked, and bread ovens were sometimes built into the masonry structure. Large castles and monasteries usually had separate kitchens, often octagonal in plan with a high roof for ventilation. Built into the walls were ovens and huge fireplaces used for different kinds of cooking; the one for roasting had spits turned either by a half-roasted child or by a parboiled dog on a treadmill.

In hot climates, hearths were often in separate structures detached from the main part of the house. Obviously a large central source of artificial heat is most undesirable in the tropics, so cooking facilities were usually in the open, sometimes in separate, rather flimsy structures. The tradition was taken from India to the Australian outback, where it was continued until recently[5] because, as well as keeping the source of heat away from the living quarters, it reduced risks of fire and vermin invasion. In areas that have a very great annual variation in temperature, the cooking place moved around according to season. In Baltistan, Kashmir, it varies from a highly insulated windowless winter chamber, often underground or surrounded by fodder, through increasingly exposed places to a corner of a veranda in summer.[6] Elsewhere, except in the largest houses, there were no separate kitchens. Cooking was usually in the main living room over the open fire on spits, or in cauldrons and kettles supported on iron tripods or on fire cranes that could be raised and lowered, and swung in and out over the flames to vary the rate of heating. Food storage was often in well-ventilated lean-tos or separate huts.

Besides fire, water is the other element necessary in all cooking. In Roman times, the urban rich had mains water. Pliny the Younger mentioned that the only drawback of his marvellous villa in the countryside at Laurentum was want of running water,[7] but there were plenty of springs or wells as sources for slaves to fill vessels from. In the first and second centuries, as well as having piped water, the rich had pools fed by rainwater from the roofs of their villas – impluvia that acted as an immediate source of domestic water; similar systems continued in the castles and palaces of the rich until after renaissance times. But, after the collapse of Roman technology until the 18th century (when here and there mains were laid out, made Roman style of hollow logs),[8] water was almost always brought to the kitchen in buckets or jars. The less prosperous had water butts: barrels for collecting roof water near the cooking place. The poorest had to rely on often long treks to collect water from the nearest public source: well, cistern, spring or stream. Much of the human race still does.

A combination of printing and respect by Renaissance architects for Classical order of the ancients (as opposed to the perceived wilful functional crudity of Gothic) generated a series of very influential text and pattern books on architecture in the 16th century. Book VI of Sebastiano Serlio's *Tutte l'Opere d'Architettura et Prospetiva*, written in the first half of the 16th century, has ideal designs for householders of every class. His great catalogue starts with 'the house of the poor peasant', which in its simplest form consists of a family room (with a fireplace) and a stable, both under the same roof. Slightly richer peasants were enjoined to build a portico in front of the hut with a bake house at one end and a cantina at the other – as in hotter countries, the arrangement kept food preparation (and consumption) apart from the main dwelling. The separation was horizontal, but in houses for richer people, Serlio usually advocated vertical division. 'It has always been my opinion,' he said, 'that houses (…) should be raised above general ground level. This is so as to give grandeur to the appearance, healthiness to the ground-floor

[3] Vitruvius op cit Book VI, chapters 4-6

[4] Oliver, Paul (ed.): *Encyclopedia of Vernacular Architecture of the World*, vol I, pp 431-432

[5] It was also common in the southern states of the US until the abolition of slavery.

[6] Ibid. pp 440-445

[7] Pliny the Younger, Letter XXIII (to Gallus). Pliny's description of his villa near Ostia is the most detailed and evocative account of domestic life and architecture in the Classical period.

[8] Usually of elm, sometimes lined with lead, and connected to individual dwellings with lead pipes. There used to be a theory that the Roman Empire collapsed because of mental degeneration due to lead poisoning from the water. Conventional economic explanations are more probable.

[9] Sebastiano Serlio on Architecture, translation Vaughn Hart and Peter Hicks. Yale, London, 2001, vol II, p 12

rooms and so as to have the commodity of the underground rooms which will provide for all the servants' workrooms (...) the cantina, the servants' dining room, the kitchen, the larder and other similar places'.[9] The kitchen was identified as a separate room, but it was banished at least partly underground where the floor above, sometimes being supported on masonry vaults, could reduce the danger of conflagration. For daylight and fresh air, servants had to rely on the whims of the owner and his architect – window size and shape depended on the composition of the elevations. In his plans of town houses for the wealthy people, the kitchen and service rooms disappear altogether, to be replaced by spiral stairs (in the poché) that connected kitchen to *camerini* or *retrocamere* from which the meal was served to the party in the *camera* itself.

[10] Palladianism was very popular in the 17th century, vying with various forms of Baroque. In Britain and its North American colonies, there was a revival of Palladianism in the first half of the 18th century.

[11] Palladio, Andrea, Book II, chapter 2. Isaac Ware's translation, 1738

Serlio's catalogue was not printed while he was alive, but clearly it plainly affected one of the most influential architectural treatises of all time, Andrea Palladio's I *Quattro Libri dell'Architettura* published in 1570. The four books were intended to publicise the Vicenzan architect's own designs and theories and, unlike Serlio's treatise, were not ideal explorations of structures appropriate for all the different levels of society. But over the next two centuries,[10] as Palladianism became the fashion over much of Northern Europe and America, the designs determined how most servants lived. Palladio believed that 'we ought to put the principal and considerable parts [of the house] in places the most seen, and the less beautiful in places as much

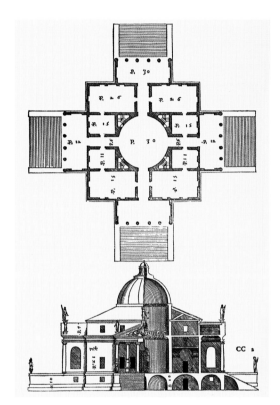

hidden from the eye as possible; that in them may be lodged all the foulness of the house (...). I approve therefore that in the lowest part of the fabric, which I make somewhat underground, may be disposed the cellars, the magazines for wood, pantries, kitchens, servants-halls, washhouses, ovens and such like things necessary for daily life'.[11] Almost off-hand, Palladio condemned generations of servants to troglodytic existence. Exceptions were in cities, particularly Venice, where basements were impossible, and kitchens were often in attics to reduce fire risks.

In the Netherlands, as in Venice, cellars were impractical, and 17th century genre painters like Pieter de Hooch show kitchens and food preparation areas on the ground floor of bourgeois urban houses or in outbuildings round the yards behind. But in English terraced housing which began to be popular a little later, kitchens were almost invariably in basements, and the servants' lot was alleviated only by areas, small sunken courts between pavement and the house which allowed kitchens and servants' quarters to be ventilated and to receive a measure of daylight. In Continental and Scottish tenements, cooking arrangements could be as primitive as those in the insulae of Pompeii but, as usual, provision varied with the wealth of the occupants and with the development of cooking and heating technology.

Illustration from Andrea Palladio's *Four Books of Architecture*, 1570: the kitchen is in the basement

[12] Leonardo da Vinci invented a version.

[13] Benjamin Thompson, born in America, was loyal to the British. He spent much of his life in Bavaria (where he became a Count of the Holy Roman Empire). His treatises, on economical and efficient fireplaces and kitchen ranges, were published in the 1790s.

Kitchens, more perhaps than other departments of the house, were radically altered by the technological revolutions that began in the Renaissance. Open wood fires remained the source of cooking heat for many kitchens well into the 19th century. But the process of roasting meat was gradually mechanised in many places, with human and canine rotating power being replaced either by a clockwork mechanism or by a smoke-jack, a vane turned by the draft drawn up the chimney by convection.[12] In the late 18th century, many new designs for cooking apparatus appeared, particularly in Britain where the Industrial Revolution was beginning. Thomas Robinson patented one of the first iron kitchen ranges in 1780. Its iron fire grate was built into the brickwork of the hearth with an adjacent oven and a movable cheek (metal plate) that could be moved horizontally across the grate to vary the size of the fire. In the 1790s, Count Rumford[13] invented a range that had a brick structure with a long stone top in which holes allowed cooking vessels to be inserted in much the way that they had been in Pompeii. Each hole had a separate fire underneath, and each fire could be regulated by varying the draft through its ash-pit door. Some have suggested that modern cookery – particularly in restaurants – dates from Rumford's invention, which allowed preparation of several different dishes at the same time, each over its appropriate level of heat. The great roasts of the great houses began to give way to a variety of comparatively quickly made stewed, broiled or fried dishes.

By the mid-19th century, developments of Robinson and Rumford's ideas were available to all but the poorest households. Mass produced cast iron kitchen ranges allowed one fire to be used for baking, stewing (in metal pans on a hot plate) and generating hot water (in a built-in boiler); irons for smoothing clothes could be heated on the hot plate, and of course the fire heated the room. Elaborate models had two ovens, temperatures of which could be adjusted separately by manipulating flues and dampers. Roasters of various kinds could be added but, in the industrialising countries where coal was becoming the universal domestic fuel (at least in cities), roasting must have been a much less appealing and savoury process than it was before a wood fire.

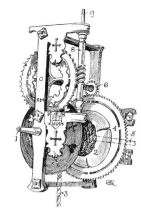

Marjorie and C.H.B.Quennell *History of Everyday Things in England*, 1918: a 17th century clockwork turnspit

Wolfgang Heimbach: kitchen interior, 1648

John Nash: Prince Regent's kitchen in the Royal Pavilion in Brighton 1826

[14] Beeton, Isabella: *Beeton's Book of Household Management*, S.O. Beeton, London, 1861, p 25

Cooking stove from Isabella Beeton's book

Isabella Beeton, whose book on household management (first published in 1861) became the domestic bible of the British aspirant middle class, argued that the kitchen 'is the great laboratory of every household' on which the health of the household depended. She laid down five principles for kitchen design: '1. Convenience of distribution in its parts, with largeness of dimension. 2. Excellence of light, height to ceiling, and good ventilation. 3. Easiness of access, without passing through the house. 4. Sufficiently remote from the principal apartments that members (…) of the family, may not perceive the odour incident to cooking (…) 5. plenty of fuel and water, which with the scullery, pantry and storeroom, should be so near it, as to offer the smallest possible trouble in reaching them.'[14] The kitchen was beginning to emerge from the basement in middle-class houses as it had already in many houses for the rich. The kitchen John Nash designed for the Prince Regent at the Brighton Pavilion (1816-1818) was a large, lofty, luminous room with a cast iron structure (in which slender columns supporting the lantern had copper palm-leaf capitals). Copper canopies drew off fumes and heat from the roasting range and, on the other side of the kitchen, from the hot plate, which was heated by a separate fire and operated on the Rumford principle.

Kitchens were often very distant from dining and breakfast rooms. In The English Gentleman's House (1864) Robert Kerr showed plans for families of different incomes and, clearly, the richer you were, the further away from the kitchen was the family table. In great houses, a separate circulation system was arranged so that servants could bring food invisibly through the building to small serving rooms that had facilities for keeping it hot before going to the table. Kerr urged a ceiling lantern for large kitchens, but in smaller ones, he settled for a big window, which ought to face 'Northward or Eastward, never Southward or Westward' to maintain coolness, so 'first that the unpleasantness of the fire heat may not be needlessly augmented, and secondly that the air may not be tainted.'[15] Kerr's ideal kitchen had a large range before which a roasting screen could be erected to heat meat on spits in the immemorial way. The range included boiler, oven and hot plate. Steam or hot water from the boiler could be piped to warm tables and serving closets, and for washing-up water in the scullery. Smaller stewing stoves were heated by charcoal. All the apparatus was arranged round the walls, while in the middle of the kitchen was a big table for preparation. A large kitchen dresser accommodated crockery and cutlery near the hot closet, and dishes were passed through a nearby hatch in the wall to the maids and footmen who waited at table.

[15] Kerr, Robert: *The English Gentleman's House*, John Murray, London, 1864 p 228

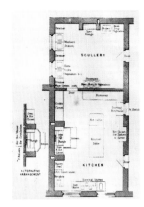

Kerr, Robert: ideal kitchen plan, mid 19th century from *The English Gentleman's House*, 1864

105

F.W. Schindler: first fully electric kitchen, Chicago World Fair 1893

[16] See for instance Parker, Barry and Unwin, Raymond: *The Art of Building a Home*, Longmans Green, London 1901. Plate 12

[17] The first electric cooker was shown at the Chicago World Fair in 1893. But electricity was not widely used in cooking until the 1930s.

[18] Beeton, Isabella: *The Book of Household Management*. Ward, Lock, London, 1898, p. 55. Coal ranges were of two kinds: closed, where the flames were concealed in a firebox, and open, where they were exposed behind a grating. In The United States, stoves of both kinds were often made on legs, and were portable from house to house.

[19] Parker and Unwin, op cit, p. 104.

[20] Ibid, p. 105

Parker and Unwin *The Art of Building a Home*, 1901. A worker's parlour with corner fireplace

At the turn of the century and at other end of the social scale, socially concerned architects like Barry Parker and Raymond Unwin were evolving flats and small houses for the poor that sometimes included little separate kitchens, but more commonly the range was included in the family living room, occasionally with an inglenook built round it.[16] But by this time, cooking with gas was becoming increasingly common in wealthy and middle class kitchens. Some of the earliest gas cookers had been shown at the Great Exhibition in 1851,[17] and by the end of the century, even the smallest towns had their local works, initially set up to provide coal gas for street and domestic lighting. The 1898 edition of Mrs Beeton (the book was regularly updated in new versions) pointed out that gas companies would provide stoves for a small annual rental. Like coal ranges, gas cookers were originally of black cast iron with polished steel handles and hinges. 'There are many features to commend cooking by gas', declared Mrs Beeton's successor editor, 'chief among which are its cleanliness and the readiness by which the fire can be lighted and extinguished, facilities which are conducive to economy. (…) Against this, however, must be placed the fact, that in the winter season, a fire must be maintained from morning to evening, and that a gas range does not present the comfortable appearance that an ordinary range or kitchener has, with solid fuel burning within its firebox or grate'.[18]

It is impossible to imagine Parker and Unwin designing an inglenook round a gas stove, but it was gas (and later electric) stoves that transformed the kitchens of the 20th century. By divorcing the source of cooking heat from the source that warmed the spaces, kitchens could be separated from living areas in even the humblest households. In the early 20th century, this became a standard way of planning, yet tenements were necessarily as economical as possible.

106

One way of reducing the price of individual dwellings was to do away with individual kitchens and adopt centralised cooking facilities. In the 1890s, Barry Parker designed several such schemes that were based partly on the quadrangular layout of the colleges of the ancient universities, themselves descended from monasteries. Parker urged that the spaces of the rarely-used front parlours of artisans' cottages should be amalgamated in a common room. 'To this Common Room could be added a laundry (…) which would take the bulky copper and mangle out of each cottage (…). [The] growth of co-operation would soon bring the common bakehouse and kitchen. From this to the preparation of meals and the serving of them in the Common Room would only be a matter of time (…). Instead of 30 or 40 housewives preparing 30 or 40 little scrap dinners, heating a similar number of ovens, boiling thrice the number of pans and cleaning them all up again, two or three of them retained as cooks…could give better and cheaper meals.'[19] Parker went on to argue that the advantages of centralised cooking could be enjoyed by the middle classes in developments where groups of houses were arranged to give ready access to a communal establishment, where meals would be supplied, laid either in the common dining room or in the private house as desired.'[20]

The notion of the communal kitchen servicing a block of flats or apartment hotel was taken up in many European and American cities before the First World War and, after it, community cooking was explored with vigour in the Soviet Union. Lenin decried the domestic slavery of women in traditional families and, in the 1920s, many proposals were made for organising society without making the bourgeois family its basic unit – one suggestion was to organise individuals by age rather than kinship. All failed, but towards the end of the decade, there were several architectural experiments in building for ideal collectivised societies. The most famous was Dom Narkomfin near the Moscow River designed by a group led by Moisei Ginsberg and Ignaty Milnis for workers in the People's Commissariat for Finances. Here, a variety of 50 two and three storey dwellings in a slab block were to be serviced by a gym, a solarium, a library, and a canteen offering prepared food made in a common kitchen by professional cooks. Dom Narkomfin was supposed to set a pattern for housing throughout the Soviet Union but, by the time it was completed in 1932, the austere high principles of Bolshevism were being replaced by Stalin's socialist-realism, which allowed more reverence for tradition in family organisation. Occupants were changed from civil servants to senior members of the Party; the communal catering seems to have worked little, if at all; Narkomfin was abandoned as a pan-Soviet model, and the building was quite rapidly converted into a block of flats for the equivalent of rich bourgeois.[21]

But the ideal of community cooking did not die out. For instance, it was drawn on by Sven Markelius in his mid 1930s Kollektivhus in Stockholm in which cooking, washing, cleaning and supervision of children were undertaken by staff employed by all residents. Flats had tiny food preparation areas, served by dumb waiters (food lifts) from a common kitchen. Though most such social experiments have failed or been radically altered (perhaps because of the now abundant provision of ready-made supermarket meals in prosperous countries), the ideal of communal cooking continues here and there, particularly in Scandinavia, where distinguished low-rise co-operative housing schemes were designed built in the 1980s and 1990s by Tegnestuen Vandkunsten and others. How far such arrangements will survive the idealism of the first generation of inhabitants is being tested.

To Christine Frederick, the early 20th century US equivalent of Mrs Beeton,[22] all such communal arrangements seemed to avoid the goal of good aspiring American middle class women – homemaking, in a single family house. Frederick was devoted to the principles of time and motion studies invented by Frederick Taylor as the basic tool of scientific management (a system for organising industrial processes under which workers' movements were measured and rationalised to reduce the effort and time required by individuals in production line manufacture).[23] Christine Frederick and her class described themselves as plagued by the servant problem, but that did not mean that they personally were free of labour. She reported that 'usually, after our dinner

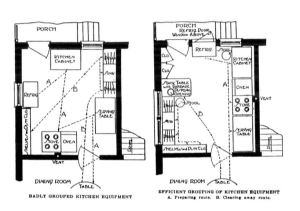

BADLY GROUPED KITCHEN EQUIPMENT

EFFICIENT GROUPING OF KITCHEN EQUIPMENT
A. Preparing route. B. Clearing away route.

Christine Frederick: studies of movement in the kitchen

I wash forty-eight pieces of china, twenty-two pieces of silver and ten utensils and pots.'[24] Using Taylorist precepts to make improvements like moving the draining board from right to left of the sink and adjusting the height of the washing up bowl, Frederick managed to reduce post-dinner washing-up time from 45 minutes to 30.[25]

Similar thoughtful analyses of domestic tasks promised great improvements in servant productivity. Frederick was aware of criticisms that Taylor's methods were inhumane and their application to the domestic scene could reduce servants to animated parts of an efficient machine for living in. So she advocated overtime payments, two half days a week off (or a whole Sunday) and, for a devoted year's service, a holiday fortnight. Such generosity was much needed when servants were expected to work eleven hours a day at eight cents an hour. (Stingy as these terms may seem, a maid's wages could account for nearly a quarter of a young professional man's salary).

In 1926, Margarete Schütte-Lihotzky, one of the first Austrian women architects, gave Taylorist principles clear architectural expression for people much poorer than those for whom Frederick wrote. Frederick believed that the lower orders could organise their own homes quite easily because they did not need to keep up appearances, Schütte-Lihotzky believed that the working class deserved the controversial benefits of Taylorism, and her Frankfurt kitchen was intended for tenants of the excellent social housing promoted by the Weimar Republic. The kitchen was created after much research into minimising movements needed to prepare, cook and wash up. Rectangular in plan (3.4m x 1.9m), it was entered at one short end and had its window at the other. Both sides had work surfaces, with the stove on the left (looked at from the door) and the sink on the right. A sliding hatch near the stove connected to the living room, and an ironing board could be folded down from the wall. There was no refrigerator but plenty of room for food storage on the right hand side. A stool on castors was the only seat.

[21] See for instance Buchli, Victor: *An Archaeology of Socialism: Ethnoarchaelogical Research at a Constructivist Housing Complex in Moscow*, Center for Slavic and East European Studies, University of California, Berkeley, Newsletter, Spring 1998, pp 3-17

[22] Or in our times, Martha Stewart – though Frederick never went to jail.

[23] Taylor was a steel man who got experience from working with the Bethlehem Iron Company. Henry Ford later applied Taylorist principles, which were supposed to help both labour (by making tasks easier to perform) and management (by making tasks quicker to perform by fewer people). In practice, they were seen to favour management overwhelmingly – particularly as they were applied by Taylor's successors.

[24] *Ladies Home Journal* September 1912, p 70. Whether she actually did this is moot, for she was household editor of Ladies Home Journal and a successful businesswoman, with interests in advertising domestic appliances. Her journal articles were collected and published in 1926 as *The New Housekeeping, Efficiency Studies in House Management*.

[25] After research, she published a table of optimum working heights for women based on their physique.

107

26 For the very rich, cooling in summer had always been a possibility since the Renaissance, for ice could be kept in well-insulated underground stores. By the late 19th century, ice saved from winter or imported from the far north could be purchased in the street and used in freezing and chilling machines.

Over 10,000 of these standardised prefabricated Type 1 kitchens were produced for Ernst May's Römerberg housing scheme, but problems soon appeared. Users had to be taught how to work their kitchens, and it was clear that they were too small to allow anyone to be in the kitchen with the cook. In an age when cooking was almost always done by women, this had the effect of separating mother and children, wife and husband. Housewives were perforce to be returned to the state of servitude from which Lenin had wished to free them. Later versions of the design were bigger with central tables that allowed two people to work together, but Type 1 defined forever the conventional individual kitchen's minimal spatial provisions and became the basis of numerous variants. Since the 1920s, new materials, new labour-saving machines and new technologies (particularly the ready availability of refrigeration and freezing,[26] and the micro-wave and washing-up machine) have radically altered cooking techniques. In most developed economies, such machines have taken on the functions that were performed by servants in middle-class houses before the Second World War. And they have altered the rituals of food preparation and consumption, for instance by making it possible for each member of a family to have a different instant meal, devoured at different times. But few innovations have had implications for domestic kitchen organisation, which tends to remain a variant of Frankfurt or of the cottage kitchen-living room, or a combination of the two.

Hasso Gehrmann: first fully automatic "Elektra-Technovision" kitchen, prototype 1970

Almost all kitchen units are prefabricated now, but that has not greatly altered fundamental planning, though many variants of appearance are available. There are a few exceptions. For instance, American breakfast bars, derived from commercial diners, emerged in the 1940s to allow meals to be eaten quickly by people either standing or sitting on high stools; they can be used as space-dividers between food preparation and food consumption areas. Another significant innovation may be the use of force-ventilated extraction hoods to allow the fire to return to the centre of the room, the place where it began so long ago, and where it is still commonly to be found in commercial and communal kitchens. In future, it is possible that some kitchens will be almost entirely automated. It is not difficult to imagine mechanisms that, at the touch of a remote control pad, could rapidly cook a wide choice of ready-made meals using combinations of freezer and micro-wave technology. They might be no bigger than a cupboard. The fire (or rather heating system) could be invisible, odours inconspicuous and labour negligible. Such things could be made easily, but after millennia of domestic cooking, I rather doubt that they will become very common, at least as the dwelling's sole focus of food preparation, for they will lack the multifarious social, sensual and versatile qualities that have for so long made the kitchen the heart of the dwelling.

Werner Sobek: Sobek House "R128," Stuttgart, 1999-2000, kitchen level

From Pot au Feu to Processed Food
The Restaurant as a Modernist Location
Wilhelm Klauser

Amuse gueule

[1] Kempinski 1997 (1997): Kempinski Hotel Bristol Berlin (ed.): Kudamm no. 27; Munich

1250 kg meat, 400 kg fish, 150 kg lobster, 100 kg caviar, 30,000 crabs, 20,000 oysters, and 18,000 bread rolls: these quantities were delivered each day in 1913 to Kempinski, a well-known cosmopolitan restaurant in Berlin's Leipziger Strasse, which served them to 10,000 guests.[1]

Entree

A restaurant is first and foremost a question of technology and logistics. It will only hold its own in the marketplace if the best and most up-to-date technologies are deployed. This makes the restaurant avant-garde. But it is not just avant-garde technologically, it is avant-garde conceptually as well: its emergence saw a sales and organisation concept that used not to exist in that form, and that has continued to develop to the present day. It is avant-garde socially, as it broke down existing social and genealogical barriers. The restaurant is the great equalizer; it gives broad ranges of people access to new experiences that were the exclusive preserve of the nobility for centuries. It is a bourgeois institution that developed after the French Revolution and manifests itself in countless variants today, matching the new social diversity, but never abandoning its basic position: a restaurant is a place where customers can eat a dish of their choice from the menu – in payment of a sum that is fixed in advance.

Plat

[2] Paczensky, Gert von, Dünnebier, Anna (1999): Kulturgeschichte des Essens und Trinkens; Orbis Verlag; Munich; p. 138

[3] Symons, Michael: A History of Cooks and Cooking; University of Illinois Press: Urbana IL; pp. 289-293

[4] Larousse Gastronomique (2001) Clarkson Potter; New York; p. 978

The concept of the restaurant is rooted in the French language. Tradition has it that it originated in Paris. In 1765, a cook by the name of *Boulanger* called the soups he sold in his soup kitchen "restaurants." He claimed they had special *strengthening* (= *restauratif*) qualities, and as well as soup his eating house offered boiled sheep's feet with white sauce. By doing this, he was infringing the laws then applying to soup kitchens organised in guilds: the guild rules did not allow caterers to sell "ragouts." Boulanger said in court that he did not cook his sheep's feet in the sauce, which meant that his "restaurants" were not "ragouts." He won his case, was allowed to carry on selling without restrictions and put up an appropriate sign over his shop.[2]

But the concept of the restaurant did not really develop until the cooks and serving staff with noble families lost their jobs during the French Revolution and had to make themselves independent, when deputies came to Paris from all over the country and were discovered as customers, and when the English fashion for eating in the "taverns" reached the French capital.[3] Antoine Beauvilliers had opened the first luxury restaurant in Paris as early as 1782, the "Grande Taverne de Londres." He introduced the remarkable innovation of listing the dishes available in his restaurant and serving them to his customers in individual portions at little tables. Until this time, all the guests had frequently sat at the host's table and served themselves from a large pot, frequently with him as well.[4] Beauvillier's guests were looked after individually, and could choose what they ate.

Raymond Mc Grath: Fisher's Restaurant, London, 1933, perspective view

Here we can see a shift towards commercial hospitality represented in a precisely regulated relationship between guest and host. "Open guesting" started to lose its significance. This was a practice available only to certain professional groups like brewers or butchers (frequently as a sideline); the rigid system of guilds and fraternities declined as well. Here in particular highly regulated environments had emerged, associated with exclusive rights for both providers and users, ultimately reflecting feudal structures. Alongside these, countless snack stalls and soup kitchens supplied a population that could not afford their own kitchens or the fuel needed to run them. Organised catering or provision of accommodation over and above this was there above all to represent the state, and was not available to the general public. It is true that some of the roots of restaurant cul-

Inn Locanda Cardinello, Isola di Madesimo, built 1722

ture, like those of all catering culture, go back to Roman times and to the Middle Ages. But these roots clearly show some organisational and infrastructural aspects going beyond actual catering that no longer have any significance in restaurants.

During the imperial period, so-called "mansiones" lined the Roman roads, a day's journey apart. These were transit guest-houses in which the empire's messengers or decision-makers could be supplied with accommodation, food and drink. This meant that the roads of the Roman empire were able to develop into an early "information network" that secured the functioning of the state. This system was revived a few hundred years later when the palatinates were established. At that time a peripatetic court often had to be accommodated and fed for months at a time. The network of palatinates was complemented by boarding houses, in which accommodation for the court was demanded from ecclesiastical and secular feudal lords. Later the church set up guest-houses in the monasteries to accommodate pilgrims or crusaders. But all these facilities were exclusive spaces set aside for specific people, and not accessible to the public at large.

112

The restaurant as a building type and independent organisation came into being only as a consequence of progressive urbanisation, increasing mobility and the transition to the modern free market economy. New social models were able to develop, and genealogical or religious rules became less significant. It was of course natural that the standard of hospitality would be levelled out.

By 1804 there were already over 500 establishments in Paris in which wide-ranging menus could be enjoyed. The cuisine became more varied at this time as well. Gastronomic reviewing became accepted as an independent literary genre and helped the new idea to spread. At almost the same time, Napoleon's conquests meant that in Europe for decades the ideal image of the restaurant, the idea of "eating" in general, was shaped by French practice. Here it was of course not just a matter of

Café Florian, Venice

Café Florian: 19th century interior

export, but also about integrating new approaches: it was not until after the Russian campaign that the bistro found a new home in France. The soldiers introduced the Russian fast-food restaurant to the French capital, where great commercial dynamism developed after 1830 as the situation settled down after the Revolution and colonies were acquired in Africa and Indo-China.

The ideals of the new age culminated in the restaurant as it had in other modern services at a time of political, social and financial upheaval. Service, decoration and interior design developed alongside culinary delights. The restaurant was a total experience ranking equally with theatrical performances, the world of illusion presented by panoramas, the goods in the department stores or the new technical worlds of the railway. "Under Louis Philippe, the private individual came on to the historical scene," said Walter Benjamin. "The private individual's habitat started to form a contrast with his place of work for the first time. (…) The private individual, who takes account of reality in the office, demands that his illusions be sustained by interiors."[5] The open fireplace, the glimpse of the kitchen and of the mechanisms of hospitality was closed off. The dining room came to the fore as a spectacular surface. Interiors from this period do tend to be reminiscent of stage sets. But the fact that

Restaurant in Istanbul

new materials like cast iron were used as well makes it clear that restaurants were seen not so much as introverted and conservative retreats, but were very firmly anchored in the present. The economic shackles were loosening, from the ordinary workpeople via the foremen, independent craftsmen and small traders to the entrepreneurs in trade and industry, but without the basic principle relating to food consumption changing: "The contrast between the two extremes is now expressed in terms of poverty and (new) wealth, in 'eating' and 'overeating'."[6] There are a lot of restaurants. Whether they are good or bad is a question of individual cultural background and thus frequently also of the diner's basic financial situation. In any case it is true to say: the eye eats as well. Staging the intake of nourishment became a special experience. Even today, ladies are seated on the banquettes in French restaurants, so that they can look out over the dining room and other diners can look at them at the same time.

Since the 19th century urban restaurants have increasingly made their mark on our towns and cities. In Germany they were bound by a large number of small-state regulations at first, and it was not until the emergence of the modern national states that they finally made their breakthrough. In a phase of high liberalism after 1870, as the consequence of an economic boom when the laws of the North German Confederation were extended to the whole German Empire, the number of bars, cafés and restaurants in Germany increased. Between 1869 and 1877 there were 31% more in Prussia, 36% more in Bavaria, 35% in Saxony, 44% in Württemberg and 28% in Baden.[7]

City statistics in subsequent years show that as such businesses increased in size, the concept became more professional and rational at the same time. For example, the number of "one-man businesses" shrank by 33% in Hamburg from 1882 to 1925, despite strong population growth, while operations with over five employees increased almost three-fold. Overall the significance of the hospitality business increased constantly in relation to other trades: in 1882 it was in sixth place in Hamburg in terms of employees and businesses, but it was already in third place by 1907.[8]

Hotels emerged close to theatres and stations, built by entrepreneurs near the new infrastructures, and promising high profits. In these places restaurants were reinterpreted as an essential component of the new, increasingly individual lifestyle, and as a possible new strategy for finding oneself, which flourished in an extraordinary fashion. The food offered and the social experience was complemented by variety, music or theatrical performances. From 1928 the "Haus Vaterland" in Berlin offered one of Europe's greatest gastronomic sensations in Potsdamer Platz, immediately adjacent to the Anhalter Bahnhof, even in the period of inflation and economic crisis. As well as a large café seating 2,500 people and an ultra-modern UFA cinema, a spectacular restaurant landscape extended over four floors. "Guests were treated to an artistic, culinary, musical and imaginary jour-

[5] Benjamin, Walter (1983): Paris, Hauptstadt des 19. Jahrhunderts; in: Benjamin, W.: Das Passagenwerk, vol. 1; Suhrkamp Verlag, Frankfurt; p. 53; English edition: Benjamin, Walter (1999): The Arcades Project, edited by Rolf Tiedemann, translated by Howard Eiland and Kevin McLaughlin; Harvard.

[6] Bourdieu, Pierre (1982): Die feinen Unterschiede; Suhrkamp Verlag, Frankfurt, p. 300; English edition: Bourdieu, Pierre (1984): Distruction. A Social Critique of the Judgement of Taste, London.

[7] Teuterberg, Hans-Jürgen (2004): Von der alten Schankwirtschaft zum feinen Restaurant. Streifzüge durch die Geschichte der deutschen Gaststättenkultur; in: May, Herbert; Schilz, Andrea (2004): Gasthäuser, Geschichte und Kultur; pp. 27-54

[8] Teuterberg, Hans-Jürgen (2004): Von der alten Schankwirtschaft zum feinen Restaurant. Streifzüge durch die Geschichte der deutschen Gaststättenkultur; in: May, Herbert; Schilz, Andrea (2004): Gasthäuser, Geschichte und Kultur; pp. 27-54

[9] Lummel, Peter (2004): Erlebnisgastronomie um 1900 – Das „Haus Vaterland" in Berlin; in: May, Herbert; Schilz, Andrea (2004): Gasthäuser, Geschichte und Kultur; Michael Imhof Verlag; Petersberg

ney round the world. To this end, circular panoramas, outstanding in their technical standard, were built up to six metres deep in some cases, giving diners in various individual restaurants the illusion they are eating in the country concerned."[9] The extraordinary expense of time and expense needed to realise and run these gastronomic landscapes did not just need appropriate financial and organisational models, increasing frequently involving banks and developers, but also an appropriate client structure that could only develop in big cities. Nothing has changed in this basic position to the present day. Modern restaurants emerge largely in cities.

Dessert

Technological progress and the division of labour this demands, was needed to make hospitality more professional. As in other fields as well, new organisational forms have reshaped the restaurant: the work had to be organised and food purchasing calculated in such a way that the product could be sold at set prices. Improvisation was not called for. Restaurants needed to rely on trained staff. It was not just working at the stove or serving in the dining room that needed specialist knowledge: working out menus, handling the accounts and purchasing also required the appropriate people. The process was boosted by technical equipment that became essential for restaurants, as they have to be able to reproduce whatever they have on offer accurately. A unique product was only of limited value in this context.

An invention by Benjamin Thompson, later Count Rumford, met a key requirement. In the late 18th century, this quirky American had provided the open fire with a double brick enclosure that took the smoke up into a central chimney, and then divided the open fire into various separate fireplaces. Each fireplace could be individually adjusted by regulating the flow of air through the ash-pit door, and pans could be placed in round apertures over each of these fireplaces. This invention meant that heat could be directed where it was really needed, and different temperatures could be exploited for cooking by moving the pans around on the hob. The ground plan was horseshoe-shaped, so fuel could be used economically and the heat controlled. Hence a dish could be prepared many times over in roughly identical quality.

But it was not until the advent of the gas oven, in the late 19th century, and the electric oven from 1900, that it was possible to cook large quantities and also meet the increased hygiene requirements. The industry developed new cooking utensils, the dishwasher was invented in the USA in about 1900. The operations increased in size as technical improvements made it possible to prepare food in large quantities with little risk involved. Canning meant that storage was feasible, and the first refrigerators came on the market. Between 1852 and 1870 Victor Baltard built the cast-iron market halls in central Paris when hygiene conditions became otherwise intolerable and the market facilities had to be fundamentally restructured. Many intermediate trading stages had evolved, and with them a processing industry. Dimensions developed that had to be thought through more extensively and comprehensively, and that started beyond the stove. A few decades after they had been invented, restaurants overtook the traditional food trade in terms of turnover. So product processing promised fantastic added value in every respect, and new traditions could be based on this. In 19th century capital cities, restaurants started providing spaces in which a new social direction mingled with innovative techniques.

DAS
KUNSTHANDWERK.

Monatlich
ein Heft von 6-8 Blatt.

Preis 20 Sgr. = 2 Mark.

Stuttgart.

Verlag von W. Spemann.

Decorative Plastik.
XVI. JAHRHUNDERT.

Essbesteck.
Kgl. Bairisches Nationalmuseum in München.

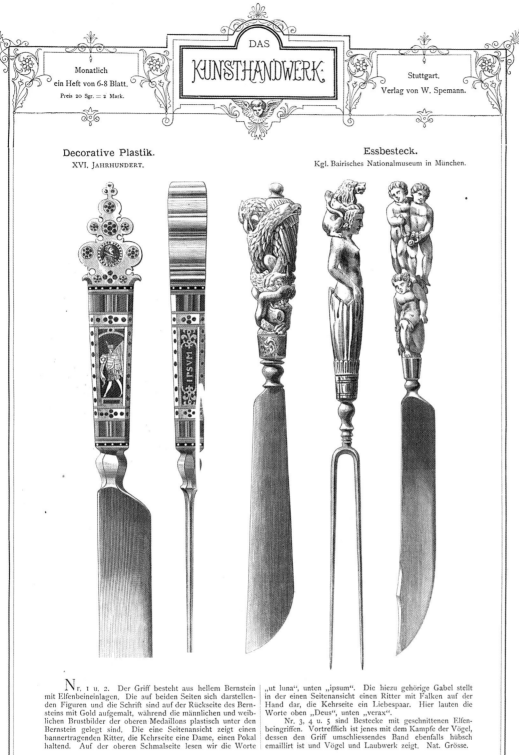

115

Nr. 1 u. 2. Der Griff besteht aus hellem Bernstein mit Elfenbeineinlagen. Die auf beiden Seiten sich darstellenden Figuren und die Schrift sind auf der Rückseite des Bernsteins mit Gold aufgemalt, während die männlichen und weiblichen Brustbilder der oberen Medaillons plastisch unter den Bernstein gelegt sind. Die eine Seitenansicht zeigt einen bannertragenden Ritter, die Kehrseite eine Dame, einen Pokal haltend. Auf der oberen Schmalseite lesen wir die Worte „ut luna", unten „ipsum". Die hiezu gehörige Gabel stellt in der einen Seitenansicht einen Ritter mit Falken auf der Hand dar, die Kehrseite ein Liebespaar. Hier lauten die Worte oben „Deus", unten „verax".

Nr. 3, 4 u. 5 sind Bestecke mit geschnittenen Elfenbeingriffen. Vortrefflich ist jenes mit dem Kampfe der Vögel, dessen den Griff umschliessendes Band ebenfalls hübsch emaillirt ist und Vögel und Laubwerk zeigt. Nat. Grösse.

Cutlery from *Das Kunsthandwerk. Sammlung mustergültiger kunstgewerblicher Gegenstände aller Zeiten*, Stuttgart 1874

Kitchen with round stove in the Kurfürstenkeller Berlin, 1926

Digestif

The restaurant has always been up to the minute. Its success made innovations possible and at the same time eagerly absorbed its own. Nothing has changed about this today. It doesn't matter whether the tables have damask napery, the plates have a gold rim or a bag of chips and a drink in a paper cup are pushed over the bar in an American fast-food restaurant: there is no place for social romanticism in this "military" organisation. The kitchen brigade works with clockwork precision. A restaurant is a business, and thus very closely linked with industrialisation. Anyone who tries to interpret the 20th century restaurant as merely a development of the rural inn, a place for socialising with a skittle alley and dance-floor attached, is making a mistake.

Restaurant growth came up against certain boundaries. The restaurateur was restricted geographically. In this context a practical solution emerged: contracting certain early stages of the work out to delivery firms. Restaurants diversified. In 1927, the Aschinger brothers were running 27 standing beer halls in Berlin, offering small dishes to be eaten quickly. To secure supplies, they built their own supply and production businesses into the empire. Over 11 million bread rolls were delivered to their own premises each day, from their own bakery.

Comparable forms of vertical integration, with the standardisation that this enabled, formed the basis for the next, and hitherto last, decisive conceptual change of form the restaurant has been through, and with which it is replacing itself to a certain extent as it moves away from the form in which it previously existed. In fast-food restaurants, it is not the speed with which people are "fed" that is the actual sensation, but the boundless duplication, the perfection of a system that makes it possible to reduce costs. Growth was achieved by multiplying identically conceived locations where identical menus could be served. The reduced profit margin on lower-priced dishes is balanced out by a correspondingly high turnover.

The fast-food restaurant removes the clear distinction between dining room and kitchen. This highly developed business model needs a different kind of space. Distances to be covered are shortened, efficiency increased and turnover enhanced. But that is not the only secret of success. Fast-food restaurants make the system visible: a view of the production process is an essential component of the marketing concept! The fact that customers consciously or unconsciously accept this radical change of ground plan shows the advance trust that the system enjoys. This gives the diner the highest possible degree of reliability and predictability. He knows what he is getting – but he also knows what he wants. Diners have long been customers who have a complete grasp of the system's strengths and weaknesses regardless of their social status and use them to their advantage.

The mechanistic design of the systems needed for fast food catering makes a "slimming diet" essential in terms of content and design in which ultimately the restaurant is superfluous, as it is a development that logically leads to "processed food." Ready meals conquered the supermarket shelves a long time ago. Customers can prepare the meals for themselves in seconds. They often have their own technical equipment nowadays that is frequently in no way inferior to that in restaurants. Here the disappearance of social intercourse and the communal experience provided by a restaurant over and above merely satisfying the appetite has to be accepted.

One for the Road...

Commodities that come under the heading "convenience foods" or "fast foods" in a market that has largely come to the end of the road try to satisfy customers in a way that is already known. This means that the range on offer no longer amazes them. Diners are not just robbed of a setting by such developments, but especially also of the possibility of performing in the presence of the unknown. A restaurant does not just offer entertainment, but is also a stage for its visitors. A diner choosing certain dishes, studying the wine list or interacting with the staff is part of a performance in the same way as the broken German spoken by the waiting staff in an Italian restaurant. Flower arrangements or interior design provide a general framework.

Peter Döllmann: MoshMosh restaurant in Frankfurt am Main, 2005

Given that diners are increasingly cosmopolitan, the surroundings will increasingly become more complex and thus also more exclusive. A kind of comprehensive design solution is emerging whereby the actually simple process of eating food is orchestrated and extended to a hitherto unknown extent.

Linguistically speaking, a guest was originally a stranger. The Latin word hostis and also the Greek xenos means "stranger," "enemy in war" or "guest," according to context.[10] Thus the guest is potentially an unknown person, penetrating what is actually a closed environment from the inside, and having to assert himself. So it makes sense to treat a restaurant as an alien and also a surprising place. And there is no question that this "strangeness" provides the starting point from which today's avant-garde gastronomy develops. This observation is certainly not referring to the many varieties of ethnic restaurant that are to be found everywhere. The döner kebab revolving lazily by its flame satisfies the customer's desire for something strange without offering any landmark solutions. It is a form of orientalism in the days of the charter flight. It needs no logistical or creative intelligence and the Germanic counterpart in the form of the "Currywurst" does not rank behind in its clear basic disposition. It is to be assumed that sushi bars will follow the same route: snacks suit one-dimensional solutions, briskly reflected in their unfussy non-requirement of cutlery.

[10] Schilz, Andrea (2004): Frühe Gastlichkeit in Worten und Fakten; in: May, Herbert; Schilz, Andrea (2004): Gasthäuser, Geschichte und Kultur; Michael Imhof Verlag; Petersberg; pp. 13-26

But the restaurant of the future will find solutions by adapting itself to a general situation by using culinary, programmatic and spatial eclecticism. A variety of hybrid solutions are emerging, mixing a large number of different interests. Restaurants are moving into slaughterhouses or discovering closed-down factory halls. Cooks are turning into writers and television stars, the menu is become a fashion or car-showroom accessory. Consumption is a symbolic everyday practice requiring appropriate spaces and attractions and also not stopping in the face of restaurants. It offers more scope for innovation than any other facility. Guests or customers don't just go there because they have to, but also and above all because of the ideas and ideals associated with it. Interest in other people and in oneself takes on ritual traits that are creatively reshaped. Complex marketing strategies stage new finance models for restaurants with the same care as a menu, an interior, music or an internet page. Of course there is a merchandizing outlet next to the cloakroom. Ultimately it is quality that will decide whether innovations will last. Ultimately the restaurant customer always has the right to choose.

Snack bar in the east harbour, Frankfurt am Main

Diner in Atlanta

The Gobalisation of Taste
Udo Pollmer

We all know that globalisation has hit our food and drink as well; it's not just branded goods from Coca-Cola or McDonald's that taste the same everywhere: menus in New York, Munich or Hong Kong are the same too, just like the clothes in the street. But "globalisation of taste" means more than just using the same flavourings. Because that's precisely what isn't working in most cases – yet.

Tastes vary, as they always have. It is easy to see why a Swiss food concern offering a tasty ready-to-serve "rat" soup in West Africa will prefer to fill the reasonably priced sachets with beef for the home market for the foreseeable future. Many products only work in other cultures after the flavours have been manipulated. Reduced hotness was essential if many Asian dishes were to succeed in Europe. But products often fail even a few villages away – because of apparently trivial differences. This happened in Germany a good decade ago: after the first flood of Western products had subsided in the new supermarkets, the customers started asking for mustard, ketchup or pickled cucumbers that "tasted Eastern" again.

Markets for convenience foods have remained regional in many ways, even when Global Players service them. The relevant firms now have up to 200 different flavouring mixtures available for the taste of strawberries alone: Tokyo and Tutzing savour their strawberries differently. Subtle distinctions between allegedly identical products present big companies with considerable problems. Even the apparently interchangeable taste of prepared seasonings by firms like "Maggi" or "Knorr" is judged differently in France and Germany. It is not a question of brand appearance, it is quite simply a matter of sensory details that customers accept or reject.

A soft drinks manufacturer's sobering experience shows how lastingly customers' perceptions and preferences are affected by things they have once learnt. He wanted to extend his range with a refreshingly clear "Crystal Cola." The main component of cola is water anyway, and the other ingredients are colourless, so all he had to do was leave the E 150 colourant out. 30 of the company's experienced tasters were allowed to try the colourless cola. But only two of them could detect the taste of cola. Over half could not even describe the flavour properly, and six thought they had a well known brand of lemonade in front of them. When a second trial was conducted and they were expressly asked whether it might be "a cola drink," two thirds of the tasters still disputed this. Later, when it was marketed, customers bought it once and once only. They simply couldn't taste it! Even minimal deviations from the standard stimulus can seriously damage sales.

Even so: globalisation is unstoppable, despite neophobia and occasional flops. The big companies will try anything to domesticate their customers' tastes. The science that deals with this, psychophysics, has been trying for years to control the "desire to eat" – and with it, sales. Flavouring firms have for a long time now been offering more than just a few roasting aromas for convenience food manufacturers or Riesling notes for waterers-down of wine, but they have now come up with taste flavour modules for "taste tuning." Psychophysicists all over the world are researching mankind's eating instincts systematically, studying tastebud responses and investigating the emotions people feel while eating. Mayonnaise is flavoured on this basis, the melting behaviour of chocolate on the palate adjusted or the crunchiness of crisps optimised.

Success has always followed correct assessment of the biological rules, studying the physiology of the body. Nibbles are a classic example. If you open a packet of crisps, it's often difficult to stop before you've eaten them all. Crisps are at their most effective when watching television. There is a simple reason for this: crisps act as a safety-valve for the aggression that forms the psychological core of many broadcasts. Then comes the next chewing phase: the material has now crumbled, and becomes soft and mushy. It nestles compliantly against the palate without sticking to the teeth. The crisp has then done its job. The eater can relax, pamper his tongue a bit with the soft mass and then swallow it down contentedly.

But for that you need a great deal of saliva, because crisps are salty and have a large, dry surface. Now the flavourings' hour has come. A common-or-garden crisp becomes a taste experience with 2-methoxy-3-ethylpyrazine. This substance has a strong aroma of freshly fried potatoes. Carefully dosed, it gives the little discs a subtle, rounded potato flavour. The typical crisps note is sounded by 2-ethyl-3.6-dimethylpyrazine. A cheap flavour enhancer like glutamate intensifies the effect of the expensive aromas and stimulates saliva production. The sound effects in the mouth and the associated jaw vibrations must not be forgotten. Crunchiness counts as an active, aggressive characteristic, stimulating you and making you want to eat more. The fact that a crisp doesn't weigh very much also boosts the desire to eat. Given how much you have eaten already, it doesn't matter whether you eat the next feather-light crisp or not. This makes it more difficult for consumers to stop.

Researching consumer reaction is the be-all and end-all for the food industry. It does not just measure the sound effects created by crisps and the elasticity of chewing-gum, but also the thickness of sauces, the fluffiness of instant mashed potato, the moistness of cakes or the creaminess of ice-cream. Even simple products like boiled potatoes are tested for friability, hardness, deformability, cohesion, rubberiness, chewability, shear force and compressive force.

The hamburger is another product that has undoubtedly enjoyed worldwide success. This is partly due to the fact that it is eaten in the fingers, which means that you can't infringe any eating etiquette, no matter what culture you are in at the time. Secondly, no one has to wash up any cutlery, and thirdly the guests can't pinch that cutlery. The slice of cucumber is central to psychophysical hamburger design. It must be crunchy, so that the customer hears when biting into it. It is

Sushi by Tengelmann (German food-chain)

impregnated in advance with the required taste ingredients like salt and acid. The ideal salt content is at least 2.2 percent, it is between 3 and 5 cm in diameter, and the thickness of the slice must be adjusted to precisely 3 mm according to the brand leader – to get the right mouthfeel when biting into it. This then releases the sweet-sour, saliva inducing sauce. The cut surfaces are toasted so that it does not seep into the roll. This means that a mild, sweetish aroma of roasting and frying is released into the eater's nose.

Why all the fuss? It is aimed – as before with the crisp as well - at our saliva flow. This unassuming word holds the key to understanding our appetite. When our mouths water, we simply have to go on eating. This is why a lot of people don't feel they have really had enough after a meal like that. This is not the fault of the soft roll, our saliva flow is to blame. If it dries up, then we feel replete. It is easy to see how our saliva can be controlled for yourself: just eat the soft roll used for your favourite hamburger as it comes, without any residual sauce. The mass coagulates into a saliva-absorbing lump in your mouth and dries it up. Precisely the opposite happens with the sauce. It draws out fresh saliva. Eaten on its own, it tastes repulsively pungent. The hamburger uses the basic principle of all food design successfully: creating more saliva than is necessary.

But there is no psychophysics that can cope with many cultural or biological differences: a Frenchman will respond to an over-ripe Camembert with relish, but it will make many Chinese want to retch. For them, cheese is nothing but a rotten, mouldy cow secretion. Many Asians are allergic to milk for genetic reasons. Their digestive system goes on strike when faced with lactose. Even the European-friendly Americans have their difficulties with French culinary practices: in the Second World War they regularly destroyed cheese dairies because they smelled so strongly of rotting corpses... So to the regret of caterers, our taste preferences cannot be manipulated at will: that is more likely to be possible if people are fed convenience foods from childhood. This effect has long been exploited for pig fattening. It is known that animals prefer fodder that contains the aromas of their first food. In piglet breeding, some sows are even fed a flavouring that passes into their milk. If the same flavouring is added to the piglets' food the young animals can be weaned sooner and the sows can be served again sooner. If animals, young puppies, for example, can be accustomed to a manufacturer's flavouring pattern from birth with a particular puppy food, then it is justifiable to expect dachshunds with "brand loyalty." Our baby food had synthetic vanillin added to it to round off the taste for many years – not enough to taste of vanilla but enough to be perceived subliminally. A study showed that adults who were bottle-fed more often prefer products containing vanillin than those who had been breast-fed.

You can't teach an old dog new tricks. Mass consumption of apple-juice drinks by children meant that convenience foods with "apple" were not allowed to taste of apple any more, but of the markedly different apple *juice* flavouring. Another phenomenon caused by first impressions of food is children refusing fresh milk because they are expecting the boiled flavour of UHT milk. Introducing new flavourings does not just affect product success or failure today, but also whether young people will ever be able to enjoy fresh apples any more. If chewing-gum manufacturers determine how "fruit" tastes and ketchup bottlers define the flavour of tomatoes, then no one should be surprised if appeals to eat fresh fruit sometimes don't come to fruition. Even if the globalisation of taste is inevitable in the long run, it will meet its limits even in future in places where our foods have physiological effects that are regionally significant. For example, chillies have a cooling effect on the body (they lower the core temperature), which is why this spice in eaten in large quantities in hot countries. In cooler areas the slightly warming effects of mustard are preferred.

So far the manufacturers' desire for globalisation has been fulfilled only to a limited extent. In the long term, baby food may well prove to have made the breakthrough. As the vanilla "case" shows, subliminal taste components can have a lasting effect on adult tastes in food. At the same time, the increasing availability of convenience foods is eroding our ability to prepare food for ourselves, and thus earlier generations' taste models as well. If the tomato sauce from mother's kitchen doesn't taste exactly the same as industrial ketchup, then the next generation is not going to see the point of making things for yourself at home. Perhaps it will not be too long before people will not need kitchens any more, because they have lost the taste for home-prepared food.

123

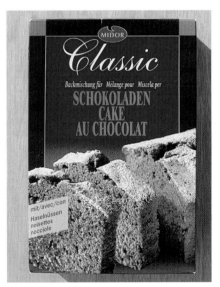

Architectural Essentials
Claudio Silvestrin

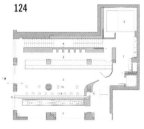

Ground plan

Both architecture and cooking conceal the essentials of life within them. In my architecture I strive to track down these essentials hidden within things and to express them architecturally. I understand the essence of architecture – and of cooking – as "lessness." Before establishing a link between my architecture and cooking, I would like to define this idea of "lessness" more precisely in architectural terms first. I think of architectural space as emptiness, as a mass of air, as depth, as silence, as something without which there can be no horizon. Space as *spatium*, as *extensio*, extending in all directions. For me, creating architectural space means in Heidegger's sense creating a place, it means placing and ordering, to retain openness. Openness, free space gives presence to the appearance of things and humans. Measured placing allows things to belong to their place and thus to relate to each other. The principle of the medieval monastery is a source of inspiration for me. Here walls create a perfect, enclosed space. When we enter a monastery, we inevitably feel the intensity of this space.

As Adolf Loos already suggested, there is no room for ornament and decoration in the search for the essential, as they prevent us from seeing timeless things, because with too much clutter, we can no longer see space. For me, contemporaneity and timelessness are both expressed in serenity, simplicity and silence, not in our day's excitements and constant clamour for something new. I am not interested in fashions, nor in what is fashionable. Thus my interest in surfaces and façades is different from that of many contemporaries. I am more concerned with the metaphysical quality of space. Other essential elements of life – water, fire and earth – join up with space. My architecture seeks to combine these elements through a clear and rigorous geometrical order and the energy that a rhythmic repetition gives – which is why it may be deemed classical.

The materials I use to create space are always chosen to reinforce that space in its reticence and its simplicity. In other words, the envelope is never a demonstrative special feature, but simply encloses emptiness. This explains the reduced range of few materials chosen, finely tuned to each other, that I use in my projects. It may sound paradoxical, but space becomes more clearly visible if only a minimum of architectural means are used. The material I use most frequently is stone. I love granite, for example: as a material, it expresses a bond with the earth, it embodies naturalness and has a primal quality. This is what I want to express. It is true that stone is worked by human hands – either roughly cut, ground or polished – and thus acquires a variety of sensual qualities, but it is not created artificially. I would never dream of using artificial materials like plastic. Plastic does not occur in nature, and can only be manufactured by processes triggered by the hand of man. I also find all the artificial protective coatings that are nowadays applied to natural materials repugnant. They conceal the tactile material's qualities.

If I choose a wooden floor, it remains unsealed. I do not see colour as an abstract term either, but as a material nature has given us. Just as my materials are "natural," so are the colours that I use. If one looks closely, nature is full of colours. By keeping to the elemental, to what nature has given us, to fundamental inherent orderliness, my architecture does not break with history and tradition, as Modernism so frequently did. On the contrary, its contemporaneity always reflects our collective,

Baker working at night in the Panetteria Princi in Milan, 2003-2004

subconscious memory as well. If my architecture is called Palladian, I take that as a compliment – even if that means that many people dismiss my architecture as old-fashioned. But in cooking – to draw a parallel – old-fashioned things are starting to be modern again.

Perhaps my architecture can best be compared with traditional Italian cuisine. This thrives on the goodness of natural ingredients. It is a cuisine without much cream and unhealthy fat, without ornament and decoration. It is simple but tasty cooking, where a great deal depends on detail. If a dish is made of very simple things, it must be perfectly prepared. If you cook a risotto, for example, you can't just say it will be ready in twelve or 25 minutes. It might need 16 minutes. Paying attention to detail like this is just as important if food is to be delicious as it is crucial to my architecture. No perfection without precision. Just as Italian cuisine is based on natural ingredients, my architecture is built up of natural elements and emphasises the inherent beauty of the materials. A simple plateful of tagliatelle – made with the best eggs and the best flour – cooked al dente, served with extra virgin olive oil and parmesan cheese, can taste wonderful. Creating something unique yet simple needs not just outstanding ingredients, but also harmonious composition. I always try to balance the elements in my architecture as well – balance without disharmony between the materials and the vertical and horizontal elements, balance between lightness and weight, between emptiness and mass, between light and shade. It is a question of proportional ratios.

125

Panetteria Princi: bakehouse, salesroom and place for eating rolled into one

The Panetteria Princi in Milan is a perfect example of my approach – especially as architecture and food are directly related here. This project fuses the life elements – water, air, fire and earth, which are crucial to cooking and baking, just as they are to architecture – in a way that makes particular sense to me. In principle the Panetteria consists of a single, large, lucidly articulated room where all the activities needed to make bread – one of our staple foods – and other baked goods, including selling and eating them, take place at the same time. Rigorous geometry is paired with warm colours and sensual materials: rough porphyry for the floor, rough stone blocks as counters and shaped as tables to stand at, earth-coloured brass panels as wall cladding, fire for baking – visible from everywhere, presented as a focal point – and of course wood, for the place where the kneading and baking take place. Baking as an elemental, primal activity, something that is normally kept from our eyes, is deliberately thrust into the foreground, spatially intensified. It happens behind great panes of glass, and can be seen both from outside and inside. The division between manufacture and selling is removed. Both take place in the same space, on the same stage. And just as all the activities are spatially linked, so are all the materials closely related to each other.

I am particularly enthusiastic about this project because it creates a space that works for everyone – despite or even because of its geometrical austerity and lack of ornaments and decoration. Here people from all social strata share the space. It is a democratic space in which everyone feels good regardless of background or status. Recalling the essential connection to the natural is not the privilege of a chosen few. On the contrary, it can still give people a feeling of stability and serenity.

126

Fire as the essential element in the bakehouse

Baked goods presented in the Panetteria Princi

The Order of Courses
A Theatrically Composed Structure
Onno Faller

A traditional order of courses follows strict, handed down patterns and ideas. Besides social status, historically established requirements and the individual conditions relating to culinary techniques, all the course components have also to be seen in the context of culinary infrastructure. Today, manual work is increasingly being done by machines, even in families who respect tradition, and the open flame replaced with radiant heat, electromagnetic fields or something similar. But the essence of the traditional menu in its sequence and dramatic structure has not been damaged by new inventions. For special occasions like communion, wedding and confirmation people like to hold on to old and familiar tastes. As the order of courses represents a precise idea of the full, correct approach, it provides a rounded design for a traditional feast that people still enjoy celebrating.

If celebratory and Sunday dishes are considered from the point of view of the time sequence of the dishes and the relationship of the ingredients of all the foods to each other, it is clear that families rely on a basic repertoire of dishes that are put together on different occasions to create a constant series of new menus. But this means that a menu defines the "edible characteristic" of a family.

What is an order of courses?

Strictly speaking, a bite of bread and butter and a sip of water already means a complete sequence of courses. Here it consists of two elements only, with a rhythm conferred by the eater himself and thus becoming a sequence of individual events with different effects: two bites one sip, two bites one sip, two bites two sips, one sip two bites etc. A menu consisting of many elements can become a very complex scenic world in which one thing arises from another, in which each part relates to the other in form and content, in which the impossible becomes possible. It has an introduction, climaxes, variations and a conclusion.

Each course in a coherent order represents a system or event that is complete in itself, relating to the menu as a whole. The more different kinds of food are offered, the more links can be created. If the menu is highly condensed, the different foods must have certain qualities in order to guarantee that things work physically and in terms of flavour. Dishes with a uniform structure, in which every mouthful is the same, like thickened soups for example, purees or porridge, require to be followed by a different experience for the mouth to satisfy the eater. Stews on the other hand, in which all the contents are there together in pieces, like carrots and meat, bacon or potatoes, can all be eaten with bread without leaving people unsatisfied or hungry. The mouth and the nose are given a lot to do with food like this, having to examine the individual ingredients appearing together before they are swallowed; you chew, grade, listen and compare. If a menu is working well, these chewing and eating experiences are so well matched that they produce a dramatic sequence with crescendos and climaxes.

Graf von Salm's table: the round table made it possible to seat a group without strict ranking and without great ceremonial. Guests who liked drinking had a cooler with a bottle of wine right by their chairs. A whole creature was dished up as food.

But each dish within a menu also has a predetermined function within a culture, as food like many other things is linked to mythological and religious ideas and to sociological patterns. They convey symbolic messages over and above their nutritional value. Meat, for example, has social significance beyond a nutritional function. For a long time it was the food of the powerful and rich. Even when it became more available in the 19th century because of modern production forms and was there for everyone, this status has not altered within the hierarchy of food ingredients. Even today, meat stands for power and strength, expresses the host's status and has to appear as the climax of the menu.

Our present menu form did not develop until the early 20th century. Before this time, food at feasts was still served in different courses, but each course included a large number of dishes. People simply ate a selection, which could not be made entirely freely. Each eater knew exactly what his status entitled him to, or what was important for his health. Unlike current menus, sweet and savoury, cold and hot food and – this was very important – examples of all cooking methods like frying, boiling, steaming etc., were offered at the same time. Today the individual dish and its order in the sequence is laid down in advance.

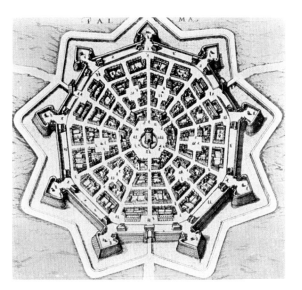

Usually hot comes before cold and savoury before sweet. All the people at the meal eat the same dish at the same time, and are thus placed on an equal social footing.

As in art, architecture or music, if a menu is looked at in terms of drama, all the possibilities of artistic effect made by an event taking place in time and space are brought into play. Architects like Andrea Palladio rebelled against the physical boundaries of time and space, gravity and mass by using Veronese's illusionist painting, and the cooks of the same period borrowed from sculpture to make an image of the world that went beyond the physical possibilities of creation. While architects created the ideal city and the ideal ground plan, the cooks constructed the ideal (edible) animal. They freed it of its bones and used sculptural methods to reassemble it as a complete creature. So the eater of

Ground plan of Palmanova

the day experienced the conditions of paradise here on earth. All he had to do was cut off a slice of meat, effortlessly. Self-confident Renaissance man even went a step further. He made models of lions from hare meat, manufactured gigantic eggs purportedly laid by terrifying monsters, or pushed artificial cushions of fat under the skins of fowl.

Artificial devices within the "building" of foods

Devices available to cooks for imposing form include repetition, contrast, variation, modulation, and these can be used as needed within a dish or a complete sequence of foods. They are the basic building blocks of any food theatre, and define introduction, climax and finish.

Pie mould from Conrad Hagger's
Neues Salzbürgisches Kochbuch,
Augsburg 1714

The choice of ingredients supplies the thematic material for the food. It can be selected strictly according to content or the type of food (meat contrasting with cereal), or following regional themes like sea, mountains, forest or field. The age of the food and the time it was harvested also contribute to form: preserved material (dried, smoked, bottled, pickled) in contrast with fresh food. Here the time aspect is in the foreground. It refers to a season, or to the transitoriness of life. Even technical achievements like fire can be conveyed by food. These themes are often introduced in terms of consistency. Soups are an ideal way of introducing main themes (meat, cereal or vegetable, or all together). They leave people curious and wanting more. Gradually the structure of the eating experience increases the tension to a point that is the culmination of everything. This can be in the form of the meat announced by the soup – now as a crisp roast – or a ragout of ingredients that have already been introduced in another form. The conclusion, usually in the form of a dessert, completes the sequence of food by adding a new, sweet aspect, and provides a lavish reminder by repeating one or another of the ingredients – now in a different gustatory context – of the spectacle the mouth has experienced.

Example of a classic order of courses for feast days from South Germany

Clear game soup
Pheasant with lentils and spätzle
Clear game jelly with lamb's lettuce and bread
Semolina slices with preserved cherries

This order of courses must date from the 19th century. It is typical of a relatively tightly organised village community, which lives within the protective bond of the family, the parish and the church calendar. This specimen order of courses makes it possible to show that each individual food within the combined dishes is by no means put together at random. On the contrary, it has a fully structured, logical form.

The selected ingredients represent the basis of the order of courses, define the "signature tune" of the landscape and the world view of the people who invented the menu. All the "material" shares the characteristic that it is found in the immediate vicinity of a South German farmhouse. The pheasant is the only wild ingredient, but it, too, comes from a cultivated situation, as it is kept in enclosures for hunting purposes, protected against its natural enemies.

Scoring the order of courses

The main point of interest in this menu is the pheasant. It appears as the only meat in three of the four courses. Comparable menus using beef or pork often include another kind of meat, or a fish. The pheasant's status in the hierarchy of ingredients is underlined by the fact that no other living creature is placed alongside it, indeed that three aspects of it are shown. As a game

131

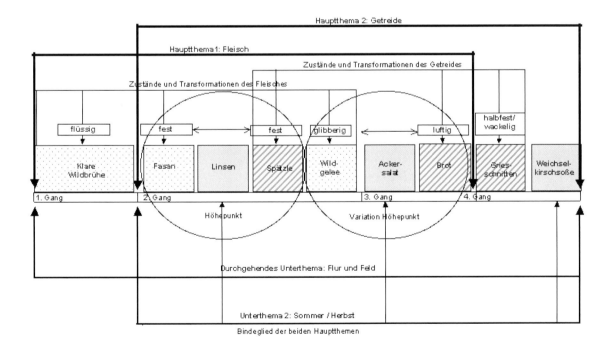

Scheme for sequence of foods

bird, it was reserved exclusively for the nobility from the late-medieval game ban onwards. Poaching was punishable by death. Even the industrial revolution, which broke down these boundaries, made no impact on the importance of game on menus. On the contrary, bourgeois cookery books from 1850 onwards increasingly include recipes for preparing game dishes.

The pheasant is cooked very slowly with aromatising ingredients like carrots, celery and root parsley, bay leaves, juniper berries and peppercorns in a large casserole with a lot of water and a little vinegar for several hours over a low heat. The quantities of aromatics are fixed so that ultimately their flavours cannot be identified individually. The bird remains in the stock overnight, thus further adding its own intense aroma to the essence. The next day, all solid matter is removed from some of the stock, which is clarified and seasoned with a little lemon zest and salt. In this form it can be eaten with bread as a complete dish. The rest of the stock is cooked for two to three more hours with the skin detached from the pheasant, its feet, head, liver and stomach, and clarified several times. After that the stock is put in a cool place. It slowly sets to a jelly because of the pheasant's rich, meaty tissue.

This mode of preparation spreads the pheasant flavour over three dishes, each with its own consistency, its own flavour, and its own ability to create an oral experience.

The span extends from

Introduction	Climax I	Climax II
clear pheasant soup	pheasant meat	pheasant jelly
hot/liquid	hot/solid	cold/slippery
savoury	savoury	savoury/sour

The rest of the ingredients are allocated to each of these pheasant-determined phases, above all the cereal elements, in the form of spätzle and bread

spätzle	bread
hot/solid	cold/airy

The dramaturgy of the order of courses

Introduction

The sequence begins with a soup plate with cold spätzle in it. The very hot, clear pheasant soup is poured over this. Only the liquid is drunk, the spätzle are not eaten. All they are supposed to do at first is absorb the pheasant flavour and warm up. So the two main themes of the menu, the pheasant and the wheat, are introduced right at the beginning: the pheasant in liquid form, but still unmistakable as a flavour, the wheat in the form of solid spätzle, but only as a visual experience at first. This concept requires great self-control from hungry guests, an essential attitude of mind at special celebrations like first communion, expressing a culture motivated by religion. But the setting – the table – is presented alongside the principal themes, and so is the "set." It is festively decorated, often in colours matching the particular event, definitely following liturgical models as well. The plate plays a crucial part in this sequence: it is not changed after each course, as it would be in bourgeois households. It is simply recharged with the next course. This custom is a relic of peasant culture, where either hollows in the wooden table or a single dish served as plates, or the pan or pot itself might even have been on the table for everyone to eat from. The "keep-your-plate" culture is in danger of dying out, as feasts of this kind are usually held in inns or restaurants nowadays, where hygiene regulations cannot admit such customs.

Climax I

The leading performer, the pheasant, makes its major appearance in the second part of the sequence. It is not dissected: the whole creature comes to the table, though the inedible parts (like feathers, head, feet, skin) will have been removed. The eye still sees it as a creature with two wings to flap, strong legs for running and a delicate breast that never had to keep the wings moving for long. But the tongue experiences the other aspect of life – death – in the form of the haut goût. These two extremes – life and death, conveyed by the body of the pheasant – are in the middle of the table at the centre of the festive company, and at the same time at the centre of the menu sequence.

Artistic innovations happen gradually in all genres, as they are always subject to evolutionary development. Culinary innovations evolve gradually as well. So the pheasant, which is a newcomer to the mixed bourgeois-peasant culture, is ultimately treated quite ordinarily in its role as a special feature in the menu sequence, in a way that is usually reserved for the long familiar pork belly.

The lentils as an accompaniment – always present in lavish quantities and making people feel full thanks to their mushy consistency – are hot, and so are the spätzle, which are already present on the plate, permeated with the flavour of pheasant. This is "real" eating, needing a physical effort (chewing properly). This course is an image of a society that still works physically, with its hands, but is already relating to other social strata.

Climax II

The second climax of this menu is another metamorphosis of the pheasant. Its essence now appears as jelly, cold and smooth. It almost melts on the tongue, and is eaten with the lamb's lettuce, which needs to be chewed vigorously, a sour dressing for the salad and the airy bread. Here the pheasant shows a completely new side of itself: greatly concentrated, without thrusting its flavour into the foreground unduly. It acts as a seasoning, and as a "stage" for a completely new ingredient, the only fresh one, the lamb's lettuce, symbolising youthful freshness. The taste of death is greatly reduced by the low temperature and the smooth surface of the jelly. The pheasant's firm, living flesh has become a cold, smooth mobile organism, and the old dried lentils from the field have become a fresh, young lamb's lettuce salad, also from the field. This course, too, thrives on chewing, on working with the teeth and tongue, on how the three components are put together, as the diners decide individually how much jelly they want to have in their mouths in relation to the lamb's lettuce, whether the bread is eaten at the same time or separately, as a neutralising agent before the next mouthful.

Conclusion

The end of the menu sequence is like an encore. Before the dessert is served the table is cleared and the tablecloth swept. Actually the meal is over, but the palate still needs something. Once again wheat, one of the main themes in the menu sequence, appears, now with a cold, solid-slippery consistency: the semolina slice. The bottled cherries handed with this add another season to the menu sequence. At the same time, the semolina soaked in cherry juice evokes memories of feeling full on carefree childhood days.

Today, menu sequences like this still crop up on isolated occasions, for a confirmation, perhaps, a first communion or a golden wedding. But traditions of this kind are increasingly threatening to die out.

134

MEAT/POULTRY/PHEASANT/WHOLE CREATURE

Pheasants originally come from Asia, but were introduced into Central Europe as game birds many centuries ago. Pheasants bred in aviaries are fat and tasteless. For a pheasant to taste good, it needs to have spent some time in the fields and meadows, and to have been shot. As prey, it symbolises a hunter-gatherer culture. According to the eater's taste, they are usually hung for a time before being cooked, so that they can develop their haut gout – a flavour reminiscent of the creature's death.

Function within the sequence of courses: The pheasant is unquestionably the most expensive ingredient in the meal. As a creature of the meadow and the forest periphery, it occupies a habitat that does not fall within the territory of peasant culture – it is an exotic guest adorning a feast day. For this reason it does not appear once only in the sequence of courses, but in three variations – variations that have become fixed concepts over the period in which food has evolved: as a clear consommé, as boiled meat and as brawn. From an economic point of view, these three dishes get the most out of the creature in terms of quantity. Boiled whole, the pheasant is first of all dissected at the table. So guests at the feast live through the act of hunting and killing symbolically. Distributing the pieces shifts the host as such centre stage. The body of a creature is eaten at no other point in the order of courses. The pheasant can be seen as the first main theme within the sequence of courses.

Historical background: All food and the ways of preparing it have been allotted to individual social classes ever since the Middle Ages. Medieval food was structured around meat, with vegetarianism playing a very minor role in the evolution of food here. Pheasants were bred in pens from the 8th century. Their meat was reserved for the aristocracy until the 19th century. Even today, most pheasants are bred artificially, reared and then released for hunting.

PULSES OR VEGETABLES/LENTILS

Lentils come from the oldest plant cultivated by mankind. The Egyptians planted them 10,000 years ago. In Central Europe, on dry, warm muschelkalk soil of Württemberg, Thuringia, Hesse and Franconia, where other crops yielded little, lentil cultivation persisted on a small scale until the end of the Second World War. Along with cereals, they provided a basis for food in peasant society, above all in the cold season, as a sauce, porridge or stew. Lentils are dried for storage, and suggest a sedentary society.

Function in the order of courses: The lentils mediate between the pheasant and the spätzle in terms of flavour. Their juicy, soft consistency makes it easier to chew and swallow both the solid spätzle and the rather dry game meat. As everyday elements, both lentils and spätzle make a familiar and above all tried-and-tested platform on which to present the "exotic" game bird. They provide certainty about flavour, and ensure that everyone has enough to eat. The lentils appear in one phase of the order of courses only.

Historical background: Lentils were an essential foodstuff in Egypt and the Near East. They were even given to the dead as food, as is shown in depictions and tomb finds from the period from 1990-1780 BC. The Bible also tells us about the great significance of lentils as food for the ancient Hebrews: Esau sold his birthright for a lentil dish, Adam ate lentils after Abel's death, and lentils were served at Abraham's funeral meal. Hebrews and Muslims ate them in memory of Abraham's hospitality and death. Even today lentil dishes are still a funeral food in some areas.

CEREAL/WHEAT/SUPERFINE FLOUR

Wheat, like the lentil, is one of the oldest cultivated plants, and has been sown since the Neolithic age. The sub-varieties seed wheat and hard wheat we are familiar with today were bred from the three varieties einkorn, emmer and spelt. Wheat today is the most important variety of cereal and the major bread cereal, and is grown all over the world. It flourishes best in an average, warm climate on moist, clayey soil and is available all the year round.

Function in the sequence of courses: Cereals represent the reliable, constant factor. In fact cereals form the basis of food in our cultural circles. For this reason they can be seen as the second main element in the order of courses. They feature in every course – in different forms and con-sistencies – according to the significance of the course and the relative status of wheat in relation to the other ingredients. In the first half of the meal they appear in solid form (spätzle), offering resistance to the teeth on a par with the meat: a kind of trial of strength for the two main themes. Both meat and cereal dominate the structure of European food. It is an interesting fact that spätzle are usually prepared so that they are harder in areas that are poor in meat, or for dishes with no meat in them. The wheat appears in a completely different form in the third course: reticent, airy and light, it leaves centre stage for the flavour of meat refined in the form of a brawn and the fresh salad. It can be transformed in countless ways, and is served in conclusion combined with milk as a soft puree. Wheat occurs in every part of the sequence of courses – sometimes in the foreground, sometimes in the background, sometimes as the main performer and sometimes as an extra.

Historical background:
Wheat too was reserved for the noble lords and ladies in pre-industrial Europe. White bread, with its refined structure and white colour was only for people involved in refined activities. People who did coarse work ate rough food with coarse surface qualities. Today a family following traditional patterns would never eat rye bread or wholemeal products rather than wheat on a feast day. White bread is still considered more refined.

EGGS/WHOLE HEN'S EGGS

Eggs are crucially important in cooking – even almost indispensable in Central Europe. They are of a fixed size, and also help to determine the quantities of other ingredients in many recipes. The egg is the ingredient that is most open to transformation by cooking: liquid when raw, solid when heated. It can be presented in any form desired, and influences and changes the consistency of other foods.

Function in the order of courses: Eggs occur once only in the sequence of courses, in the spätzle dough. Visually they can be detected as such only through the slightly yellowish colour of the spätzle; they do not dominate the food in terms of flavour either, but reveal their presence to the senses of chewing and biting by giving the spätzle the right consistency. The ratio of eggs to flour determines how much the spätzle will resist the teeth. The high proportion of egg in the spätzle dough does not express prosperity, but shows an effort being made to give the cereal roughly equal status with the meat in the mouth.

Historical background: The domestic hen was bred from the wild Bankiva hen about 5,000 years ago. The Romans brought domestic hens to Western and Central Europe. In the Middle Ages it was monks above all who kept alive the culture of keeping hens. Charlemagne passed a law to distribute hens among the peasantry in about 800. So they have been part of the typical farmyard repertory for centuries, and are still an important source of meat and eggs today.

MILK/COW'S MILK

Milk provides nourishment for calves. In recent decades it has replaced human mother's milk for a large proportion of the population by being transformed into powders with the fat artificially removed. It is used fresh in the kitchen mainly for sweet foods or porridges. Children's food in particular is often cooked with milk. For this reason milk is always associated with childhood. The production of cow's milk requires grazing land or cultivated food.

Function in the order of courses: Milk's image as children's food can also be seen in the sequence of courses. It is boiled with the wheat to a very slightly sweetened porridge, but served cold, thus marking the end of the meal with a completely new and effortless flavour and chewing experience.

SALAD OR VEGETABLES/LAMB'S LETTUCE

Common lamb's lettuce or corn salad is actually an annual wild herb, to be found in ploughed fields and verges, but it is also cultivated in domestic gardens.

Function in the order of courses: The lamb's lettuce is the only raw ingredient in the order of courses. If it is to retain its crispness, it must be cleaned as soon as it is harvested and eating immediately after being dressed. It takes on two roles: it symbolises youth, and thus awareness of the past, and indicates the season in which the meal is being eaten. Lamb's lettuce can be harvested from early October to Easter. So this meal is being served in the cold season. In peasant household, lamb's lettuce was often the only vegetable available in this period.

FRUIT/STONE FRUIT/CHERRIES

Sour cherries – ripe even in the early summer – can be kept in sugar with air excluded for two to three years, with their colour darkening each year.

Function in the sequence of courses: The cherries introduce mental images and memories of high summer into the meal, and add the meadow scattered with fruit trees or the orchard into the meal as the last landscape sphere. In terms of flavour, they create tension between the delicate (baby) porridge and a fruity, aromatic sweet-sour quality.

Historical background: Preserved fruit symbolises man's sedentary nature. Having fresh fruit available for as much of the year as possible is part of a reputation of being worthy of one's class. Deep freezers and the current availability of almost all foods all the year round are contributing to the gradual disappearance of the taste experience of fruit preserved in sugar.

Slow Food
Carlo Petrini

In the late 1980s, a group of inspired gastronomes in the little Piedmontese township of Bra started a movement committed to protecting our right to enjoy good food. The Slow Food manifesto is devoted to criticism of the speed of our soulless world of machines and heavy industry. The young Bra group sets a new philosophy of life against contemporary life models, aimed at encouraging people to return to slower lifestyles built around good food in pleasant company. Slow Food represents an act of rebellion against a civilisation based on the sterile concepts of productivity, quantity and mass consumption, destroying habits, traditions and ways of life, and ultimately the environment.

The response to these themes was a slowly spreading movement that has finally reached millions of people with its inherent political, social and economic themes. It is in fact possible to say 20 years later that the movement with all its various aspects has contributed to consolidating the original brilliant idea that a future that is worth living in is only possible if it works on the sustainability principle and makes everybody happy.

We now know that sustainability is the only viable answer to today's complex, systemic and controversial world. It may be simple to put forward ideas that become common property in time, and can even be abused, think of the Greens, for example, who have been proclaiming the idea of sustainability for almost 30 years without much success. But it is more difficult to start up the kind of virtuoso mechanism that transforms ideas into reality and at the same time constantly gives them new leases of life. Creating these links and taking self-fertilising, growing knowledge further as a basis for new impulses and viable projects is now Slow Food's task. To understand this better it is worth remembering some of the stages in the evolution of Slow Food.

The story of Slow Food begins with the highly controversial opening of the first restaurant in the McDonald's chain in Rome's Piazza di Spagna in the 1980s. Placed in one of Italy's most beautiful locations, a showpiece for our country throughout the world, it became a symbol of invasion by an alien culture, bringing with it a levelling and production-promoting attitude. The

Piazza di Spagna and the idea of the beautiful conveyed by the steps and the historic palazzi around them were violated by shop windows and yellow Ms, exuding an ominous stench of heartless food, fried unhealthily. Good taste and delight in beauty were threatened by the oppressive presence of these enormous yellow Ms, the symbol of the chain. The founders of Slow Food did not want to give in as if faced by an inevitable event. On the contrary, they tried to persuade people that Italy's and the world's wealth lay in culture, and in local traditions that had developed over centuries. Starting with ideas that have nothing to do with food at first, the movement drew on a line of thought that is a simple as it is forgotten: that our food is culture. But a living culture is determined by the rules of taste, in harmony with the seasons. It corresponds with the complex variety of the territory and changes with historical events. It did not need much for this idea to spread: the Italian Union came into being in 1986 and Slow Food went international with a congress in Paris as early as 1989.

The early years were used for mobilising personalities and students of gastronomy, to whom scarcely any attention was paid at the time. The aim was to find producers whose whole heart and soul was in their products. These products later became the subject of tastings, they were presented at markets and trade shows, and introduced in newspaper articles and books. All this was done to familiarise the public with the idea of a necessary diversity to replace uniformity, to explain the importance of detail as opposed to bolting a meal down on sterile premises and to point out how important it is to know a cheese and its origins, the various manufacturing stages it passes through and the places where it matured.

The first taste education initiative came a little later, aimed at both adults and children. After this, events where rare foodstuffs could be found were organised, and these were joined by the "Ark of Flavour" project. Put pictorially, we took all the products that were threatened with extinction on board the rescuing ark, harried by an economy that would leave no room for them: cheese, sausages, vegetables, fruit, kinds of meat. Historical studies were carried out, fishermen, cattle breeders and farmers interviewed who had made it possible for these rare products to survive, and photographic records were made. As well as this, Slow Food made efforts to form an association that would bring the producers together with vets and farmers, to establish production guidelines, devise its own economic strategies and create efficient alliances: this led to the Slow Food Convivia, bulwarks of bio-diversity.

139

Going beyond gastronomic products and traditions, the international association's cultural revolution meant the transition from the plate to the field, as it were. Enjoying a particular kind of food implies knowledge, but also an attitude of mind and special, irretrievable experiences. All this is part of our life. Eating a deep-frozen fish on the fifth floor of a building is completely different from savouring it on the seashore, prepared according to regional customs and to a certain extent under the eye of the fisherman. It is about the holistic quality of the foodstuffs. Marvin Harris coined the wise saying: "good for eating, good for thinking." And in the words of the farmer-poet Wendell Berry, this means that "eating is a peasant act." Put in concrete terms, this makes eating a political act for Slow Food, identifying those people who stand for sustainable development, maintaining traditions, defending the environment and bio-diversity, for respect of identity and social justice.

Food brings the whole world together. Our civilisation developed over centuries, and now seriously threatened in its diversity by industrialisation, is brought together in food. Any food must contain the full quality of a product. But what does quality mean when applied to foodstuffs? For Slow Food, an ingredient is of good quality so long as it meets three requirements: it must be good, clean and fair. Each of the three categories is equally important, and none can be omitted. In this context, good means valuable from a biological and a sensual point of view. Clean means sustainable, which means that a product must be produced using techniques that do not pose a threat to eco-systems and soils, that respect bio-diversity and create a healthy ingredient. As well as this there is an element of social sustainability, which must be taken into account. This is covered by the "fair" category. Food must be ethically sustainable. Manufacturing methods must not involve any exploitation of the producers involved. Prices must be appropriate, and they must be appropriate not just for the consumers, but also for the actual producers, whose survival depends on the manufacturing process and who should be appropriately rewarded for their work in both social and economic terms.

Good, clean and fair: three essentially simple categories, though they may well severely restrict the selection of really high-quality products. Even so, the food must meet all these three criteria. Seen in this way, gastronomy becomes a holistic science, including agriculture, economics, the political and social sciences, anthropology, engineering etc. Food accordingly becomes a synthesis of science and tradition. A basis is forming in the name of the newly defined quality for an overall standard that does justice to good taste, social justice and the environment, and whose criteria can also be applied to the various social aspects involved – as the driving force behind a lifestyle that is taking up traditional things like old tunes, dances or dialects. And indeed people talk about "slow life," about a "slow" approach to life when they want to identify something that is not folklore, but derives from the people in the manner of folklore, in the sense of folk culture, popular knowledge. Folk knowledge, matured over centuries of trying out, experimentation and conceptual testing, forms the basis of a new culture that is closely linked with the reality of things. Slow Food today means responsible practice, precisely speaking, bringing back the good old days and also adopting a sensible attitude to modern science that does not allow itself to forget that it is at the service of mankind. In this sense slow is an appropriate attitude to the things of the world, whose resources are necessarily worth sustaining, as it involves economics, international co-operation and territorial projection.

Slow Food stands up for smallness of scale, for human dimensions, for dialogue and for commitment, for the quality of things. Slow food means rationality and simplicity, without forgetting that being serious does not mean being sad. In the words of the Italian singer Vinicio Capolessa: "Slowness is aristocratic and nobility is obligatory." Good taste means all this: how you live, where you live and why you live.

Sandro Botticelli: The Wedding Feast 1483

A Visit to Raymond Blanc at *Le Manoir* or
A Culinary and Architectural *Gesamtkunstwerk*
Petra Hagen Hodgson

A dead straight stone path, luxuriantly fringed with lavender, wraps us in bewitching fragrance and leads us to an imposing English 15th century country house: the restaurant and hotel *Le Manoir aux Quat' Saisons*, just outside Oxford. Raymond Blanc, my host, welcomes us cordially in his tiny, unassuming office in the attic of the extension, which is not immediately recognisable as such at first, as its architectural language sticks very close to that of the existing building. Raymond Blanc talks enthusiastically for almost two hours about his childhood in a little village near Besançon, about his personal background, his vision, his house. And almost in passing this explains how his life's work came into being: the idyllic *Gesamtkunstwerk* – total work of art – that is *Le Manoir*.

"At home the table was always the heart of the house, the centre of the family. We talked here, ate, quarrelled, laughed. On Sundays there were always as many as 15 people. We children weren't allowed to leave the table, we had to stay there for the endless arguments about politics and religion, longingly waiting for the crowning glory of the delicious meal, the mousse au

Vegetable garden and orchard at Le Manoir

chocolat." Raymond's grandmother had a large garden with fruit trees and vegetable beds. She was well known locally for her distilled liqueurs, and cooked well and inventively, as did Raymond's mother. His watchmaker father taught him precision and perseverance. He had built the family home with his own hands. On the side, he was a passionate amateur gardener. The son always had to help him. That's how he learned how to mix concrete, saw wooden timbers for the roof, dig the garden, water, harvest the fruit and vegetables. Father and son brought seasonal produce home from the nearby woods in the bleak countryside – the countryside that Le Corbusier also grew up in – fished for trout in the streams, caught frogs and collected snails. The family had no refrigerator. The women preserved and bottled. The deliciously promising jars stood row upon row in the cellar. The young Raymond learned to be deeply attached to nature, to the seasons and the essential things of life. Later he was thrown into the world of rational thought, passed his school-leaving examinations and ended up at Besançon Technical College, miserable as sin. At the age of 20 he tried to decide what he felt called to do: "Mathematical thought was not for me, but I knew that every one of us has a talent, I just had to find mine. It doesn't matter what I do, the important thing is to put my whole heart into it." He tried out all sorts of different things, and hit upon cooking by chance. In the Place de Victor Hugo in the middle of Besançon is the *Palais de la bière* restaurant. Raymond Blanc was magically attracted to this theatre of community life. Here, under the trees in the town square, and in the more intimate candlelit interior, a romantic picture of French life opened up.

The magnificent Great Milton Manor

Raymond Blanc washed up the glasses in the *Palais de la bière* for months, polishing them till they shone. He learned how to look after guests, and worked himself up to the position of Demi Chef de rang. At nights he cooked for his friends, several times a week. This was his actual schooling. "Knowing your trade," says Raymond Blanc today, "is essential for everything. Ideas and creativity alone are not enough. You need a structure, a solid foundation, a basis, even if acquiring it can often be very boring." He made his way to England to learn the language. Here, he was allowed to get at the stove in the *Rose Revived* restaurant in Newbridge, and refined his tastes. He opened the first restaurant of his own in Oxford in 1977, next door to a women's underwear shop and a Salvation Army charity shop. It very quickly became well known, and won its first Michelin star, and then a second. Five years later he bought the somewhat dilapidated *Great Milton Manor*, with financial assistance from friends. He built up the house to be one of the leading hotels and restaurants in England, working above all with the interior designer Emily Todhunter, and proceeding with utter single-mindedness, a sense of craftsmanship and extreme delight in being there for other people, for living hospitality.

Raymond Blanc's culinary memories of his childhood have always remained the benchmark for his own cuisine, even though he now cooks on a different plane. "My mother's cuisine was built on the freshness of her ingredients. It was simple, light cooking with clearly structured flavours. People often mistakenly compare everyday cooking with Haute Cuisine. Both can be outstanding – given a good cook. But it is just as impossible to compare them as it is Agatha Christie with Oscar Wilde, the Rolling Stones with Hector Berlioz, the architecture of a simple home with that of a cathedral. Everyday cooking prepared with craftsmanship offers direct, simple pleasures. Haute Cuisine means culinary refinement, created with exquisite craftsmanship, great talent and a bold imagination. It achieves apparent simplicity through complexity, harmony through polarity and freedom in restriction. Of course it is just as dependent as any other cuisine on the excellence of the materials used." The massive spread of industrialisation in England after 1945 meant that many farms could not survive the fierce competition and had to stop producing food. Raymond Blanc often found it impossible in the 1980s to find the right ingredients for his cooking.

He thought back to his grandmother's kitchen garden and developed 30 acres of land belonging to his country seat into a large vegetable garden and orchard, working on organic cultivation principles. This now supplies all the restaurant's vegetable ingredients for eight months of the year, providing over 90 different kinds of vegetable and 70 varieties of herb. "But first of all I had to change the gardeners' apathetic attitudes, before I could really build up the garden." After years of rationalisation, standardisation and a horrifying reduction in the range of fresh products offered, Raymond Blanc now believes that we are gradually going back to fundamental values. He thinks people have now had enough of tasteless peppers, unripe pears, polluted eggs and battery-farmed meat that tastes of nothing. He is sure that the alarming increase in obesity, the scandals about BSE and other diseases of civilisation in the context of bad eating habits will gradually rekindle increasing awareness of high-quality, healthy and at the same time tasty food. The increasing coverage of culinary subjects in the press and on television supports this. For Blanc it is out of the question that there might be a "ferment" in all social classes. In the longer term, he thinks there will be a revival of local production, not just aiming at shareholder value, but meeting the wishes of critical and informed consumers. Blanc, who is convinced that good education is crucially important, finances a young people's scholarship, writes prize-winning cookery books and has set up a cookery school at *Le Manoir*. Modern people don't want to construct elaborate, lavishly decorated cakes any more. Life is too short to stuff a mushroom. They don't want to eat heavy sauces or be confronted with flavour overloads. So Blanc's school deals with fundamental craft skills, knowledge of materials, a sense of producing clean flavours, simplicity, time management, organisation, healthy living. If the individual dishes on a menu are well matched, they are not just tasty in culinary terms, but also easily digestible.

He is relaxed about fears that globalisation will have a negative effect by levelling tastes down world-wide and causing a loss of traditional, regional cooking. When Blanc uses lemon grass from his garden in his kitchen, he sees it as an inspiration, as a way of exploring undiscovered worlds. Once the potato was an exotic fruit for Europeans, and the now omnipresent pepper a strange spice. The essential thing is to be rooted in your own traditions, being at home in your own culture. Blanc uses cardamon seeds, chilli peppers, ginger and turmeric, but *Le Manoir* still remains completely French. Herbs and spices lend flavour to a dish. Blanc points out that they

Laid table with starter at Le Manoir

144

should be used circumspectly, so that they do not start to mask the flavour they are actually intended to reinforce. "Cooking," says Raymond Blanc, "follows rules and measures proportions carefully, but it is not science: it is a mixture of experience, intuition and creativity. The strict rules laid down by the likes of Escoffier led to conformity. Nouvelle Cuisine turned against this, with a slice of kiwi fruit on every plate symbolising "lightness" and "originality." But Nouvelle Cuisine downgraded cooking to an art for the eye, rather than one devoted to taste. "Like modern architecture, Nouvelle Cuisine separated the roots from the tree. All it had to do was prune the tree so that it could grow better."

Spices in the Istanbul spice market

The Cuisine of Making Shelter
Ian Ritchie

We are neither robots nor part robots. We are human beings. We have senses and yet few architects appear consciously to design to engage with them, other than sight, sound and, to a limited extent, touch. However, the aesthetic dimension ought to include all our senses – not just the classic five but also the feel for balance mechanisms and internal sensors such as pressure. In recognising things that please us we bring several senses into play simultaneously. Food can be a visual delight, but we have also to feel texture, taste, and temperature and most importantly smell, in order to appreciate it fully or detest it. Take their sense of smell away and people lose interest in food.

Knowledge, skill and understanding are crucial to begin imagining what we might construct. To me, the advent of *Nouvelle cuisine* with its light, elegant and simple dishes mirrors an architectural movement that was evolving towards a minimalist structural expression of tension and compression and the individual elements that made up the buildings – consequently seen as a stylistic expression of technology. The rupture with tradition in many aspects of our culture – theatre, music, painting, sculpture, writing, cooking – has today given us a rich pluralism. The 20th century utopian dreams may be dead, but investigating what is actually happening and searching for a better outcome for the wider community is certainly not. There exists a freedom of creative and personal expression today. Yet none, in a traditional aesthetic evaluation, is any better than the other. That is not to say that one form of expression may not excite our senses more, but this may be fairly superficial in that it simply amuses or appeals to us more in a rather selfish way.

My conceptual thinking has always been open to allow the synthesis of art, science, technique, landscape and economy with a concern for the environment and social purposes. For the last two decades, I have been trying to find ways in our architecture to reduce energy in the manufacture of products through working closely with industry to achieve less energy intensive methods of producing. My office continually attempts to improve the thermal performance of buildings with less dependency upon implanted energy systems, and we always take account of the manner in which the building(s) are planned to benefit from the environment and to contribute positively to the urban or landscape context. Currently, I am trying to find solutions to significantly reduce the maintenance of the buildings. This has led to using naturally ageing and decomposing materials which have a long life. They include quarried, un-machined stone (gabions); naturally oxidising steel (Cor-ten®), woven bronze wire cloth to use less material, and materials that we have not been considered hitherto to be of high enough architectural quali-

Terrasson Cultural Greenhouse, Terrasson-la-Villedieu, France, 1992

ty, such as sustainably-sourced plywood. We also embrace the use of materials less-processed by industry, thereby reducing energy consumption, cost and maintenance; materials that have achieved architectural design value despite their basic nature – as illustrated by the Terrasson Cultural Greenhouse designed in 1992. The de-processing of architecture truly appeals to me. My desire to find new ways of making architecture and achieving better ends in a broad sense still leads to developing and exploiting new combinations of materials and fabrication techniques. However, all of these approaches and ingredients are, in the end, measured by bigger questions of economy, efficiency and the aesthetic values within the society where we make architecture. So, in which way is a particular society and a global one likely to develop? Cooking as analogy supports the historical idea of locality – of place and region, and a relationship between architecture and cuisine can be argued since both evolved from and nurtured local culture. If culture is raising our horizons above survival, then cuisine and architecture must invoke, apart from healthiness, above all pleasure and delight.

Is there a synthesis of science and ethics combined with man's creative desire and need to express himself unselfishly that could give us a new paradigm in architecture and urbanism? This would oppose a superficial and selfish architecture that appears too often to gratify itself today on hyperbole. Intelligent, unpretentious and socially orientated architectural expression capable of the most marvellous and spiritually uplifting structures should be able to confront such turn-of-the century stunt-making architectural and engineering gymnastics. This is a genuine challenge in the face of an insatiable appetite for "the new," "the different" and "the unique image" that still drives the present architectural scene as much as economy – to me an outdated notion of progress and of the society of the so-called developed world. This challenge has led me to ask basic questions as to what will be the important ingredients of good architecture in the future. I've explored three of them in this short essay.

1. How does our intellectual heritage shape our actions?

I believe that our present discomfort of having to live with apparent contradictions lies in the unhappy split between body and soul, spirit and matter in Western thinking, i.e. in a *homo sapiens* that needs to find ways of taming a rampant *homo faber* and *homo consumeris*. Rather than finding ourselves at one with nature we developed – since Greek times – towards a world where man thought himself more important than nature. This separation was tellingly reflected in the Bauhaus' wish to integrate beauty and reason, art and technology, freedom and necessity. In other societies, there had never been such an apparent split. Buddhism or Taoism for example do not know such a split. Their way of living includes the cyclical nature of change, something the West should in my view integrate more deeply into its own way of life and with it also into architectural thinking.

Technological innovation has always remained the driving force behind development. In the 1960s the phrase "technology is the answer, what was the question?" became in the 1990s "architecture is the answer, what was the question?" To me, this level of simplification does us a disservice. Architecture, if it is about improving our built environment and our well-being, is a more complex issue. It is not about style or fashion, or producing mimetic architecture reflecting some newly discovered pattern in nature but about making the very best of the resources *to hand*. And these resources – people, land, water, air, materials, light and energy – are the future prime ingredients of architecture and using them more intelligently – environmentally, socially, aesthetically – should in my view help to build a more civilised world.

The context of these resources varies. The anthropologist Stanley Diamond suggested that civilisation may be regarded as a system in internal disequilibrium; technology or ideology or social organisation are always out of joint with each other. This contributes to the idea of progress. And this is why designing a better future is so challenging. At the same time it questions how we make use of the big resources at our disposal – economics which should be seen as a way of better managing the world's resources, not as a mechanistic means to exploit; politics and the direction that it can take society, which is increasingly understood as a global one; and technology and its true impact and value.

Natural History Museum, Ecology Gallery, London, 1989

The paradigm I am referring to is evidently more than some architectural style and more than a conventional notion of sustainable development. It has to recognise a world that has already become appallingly urbanised, where money rather than people is more valued, and with little evident idea of our shared humanity. For those of us living in economically powerful post-industrial societies it is about a fundamental change in the way we think, behave towards each other, design and make things. It is how we act, which is how we make culture. Understanding and taking account of the indirect and hidden dimensions (light, sound, smells etc.) will become an ever increasing responsibility of the designer as we densify and try to keep our cities habitable. These hidden dimensions together with those that we can see will determine the future quality of life. We have to get our cities right at the micro-level.

In 1989 we designed the Ecology Gallery at the Natural History Museum. This was the first time that I consciously investigated reaching senses other than sight and sound and avoiding poisonous materials. The crystalline white glass walls suggested a very fragile environment. The sheets were fixed in such a way that sound resonated when the sheets were tapped. The entry floor was made of recycled rubber – soft. Each bridge had a different tactile surface identifying the history of man's manipulation of materials – wood, metal and glass. A twin cherry handrail is the only connecting element – its tactile surface shaped to the hand and forearm.

2. What are we thinking about today?

Our individual and collective thinking is sandwiched between a moral environment full of bureaucratic rules and regulations telling us how to behave (and to design) and a moral vacuum where international agencies acting on behalf of our conscience cost us the occasional coin dropped into an Amnesty or Greenpeace collection box or envelope. We are, ironically, becoming less responsible for our lives. In the West we have become the product of our own economic thinking to the point where financial reward can be obtained from being irresponsible, from not caring for others or our environment; where the largest incomes are with those who entertain us, or those who gamble best. The decline in the only life-long relationship we really have – the family – is paralleled in the rise of an increasingly contractual and litigious social world. The quality of life is strained, and the vast majority of people cannot choose or control it. This leads to alienation and loneliness. Not in the sense of not having people around but in the sense of seeing ourselves as more than vessels of blood, held together by bones and skin – vessels containing a spirit of life that may suggest to us an idea of the point of life; a point or moment when life gives us a sense of its richness, of meaning or value. How can we re-orientate to move forward and how can architecture contribute?

3. How are we behaving as designers?

I believe that for architecture it is paramount to look at how we educate architects. Leaving aside the ingredients for a moment, most architects are educated through the "design crit" system. It is here that selfishness, aggression and a defensive pose in architects is too often born, even nurtured. Rather than to gain a deep knowledge about social context, materials, construction technologies, the employment of light, in short, the things that make up the essence of architecture; and, rather than creating a sense of a shared journey – learning and discovering, synthesising and assembling, the design crit, in my view, isolates individuals more and more into a competitive, master – slave and non-collaborative mode of working which takes years to undo in order to create genuine respect for others, including the community, and their values in the creation of our built environment. Working along-

Stockley Business Park, London, 1988

side other professionals is nothing like the same as working *collaboratively* with them. I believe strongly that we need to apply our knowledge much more intelligently than to litter our world with selfish architecture that does not care about its surroundings or its impact for the environment nor about true needs for people. As designers we know that we should have a moral obligation to far more people and to the long term well-being of the environment than simply our paymaster.

Much of architecture today is simply designed for the eye. We take far too little account of all our other senses and our intellectual awareness of social and environmental responsibilities. Light is *the* material of architecture through which we can best design, and best appreciate the nature of space, surface, textures, colours and forms. Usually a view or need informs the placing of a window or opening through which light enters rather than a desire to allow light itself to energise the space and produce atmosphere. I believe that the history of architecture is a story of the way light enters buildings and reveals form and that different cultural sensitivity to light is central to architectural differences. The question of how light penetrates space, shapes it and alters it by means of shadows will always interest an architect. This is the cuisine of making shelter.

149

It is with the quality of the ingredients, their preparation and the manner in which they are put together that allows cooking and architecture to be great art. Thinking, writing or designing and creating architecture always starts and concludes with the potential atmospheres that you have been invited to create; whether they are felt from outside, as part of a city, or inside. My architecture starts in the spaces I create in my mind, and these are as much from reflections, dreams and imaginings as they are from trying to make the best visual forms for my clients with my eyes.

Copper:

A better understanding of the processes from extraction to coil helps to use this material in new aesthetical ways, exploiting the different quantities of copper ions that run off over time when the copper is left un-patinated, or post-patinated or treated with anti-graffiti coating; and how these ions "lock" into the mineral surfaces around. Another form of using copper is by using less of it in the form of woven phosphor bronze wire, and the soft, tactile qualities that this can give to architecture.

Steel:

Allowed to oxidise naturally as in Cor-ten® steel is first bright ginger and turns over slowly to a burnt red. It is a steel that is not visually shiny and hard, but has a visual softness, requires almost no maintenance.

Stainless steel:

Shot peening stainless steel creates a more durable and resistant surface and also changes its reflective properties, rendering its surface very responsive to changing light.

Metal:

Most metal buildings I have experienced have not considered touch – and have never been designed to be leaned against. The machined, controlled line and hard surface aesthetic does not have to be the only product of industrial metal manufacture. In the Plymouth Theatre Royal Production Centre we have realised soft metal rainscreen wrapped buildings. Manufacturing processes can give us soft and less controlled surfaces. And choosing materials that allow the environment to change the surface is an aesthetic design decision which embraces not only the appearance, but becomes a metaphor for designing with rather than against nature, of beginning to unwind the long recent past where everything we have created becomes everything to be maintained.

Gabion:

Gabions are caged rocks. They capture the feel of non-linearity. It is the non-repetitive forms of the stone – a collection – the collection of individual fragments from the same geological time tied together by wire. Even the wire has a pattern that the rocks interfere with, leaving it structured yet random – no two cages remain visually the same. The earliest known use of gabion-type structures was for bank protection along the Nile River about 7,000 years ago. The gabion system has evolved from baskets of woven reeds to engineered containers manufactured from wire mesh. The lasting appeal of gabions lies in their inherent flexibility. Gabion structures yield to earth movement but maintain full efficiency and remain structurally sound. They are quite unlike rigid or semi-rigid structures which may suffer catastrophic failure when even slight changes occur in their foundations. Gabion efficiency increases rather than decreases with age. They are a product of designing with nature.

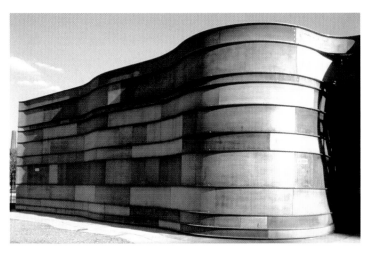

Bermondsey Underground Station, London, vent shafts, 1998

Plymouth Theatre Royal, 1997

Crystal Palace Concert Platform, London, 1996

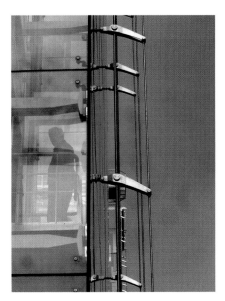

Centro de Arte Reina Sofia, Madrid, 1989

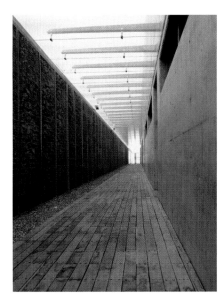

London Regatta Centre Club- and Boathouse, 1993

Biographies

Renate Breuß, b. 1956 in Hohenems, Austria. Freelance art and culture historian; teaches culture and design at the *Fachhochschule Vorarlberg*, media design course from 1999; seminars and lectures with numerous publications on cultural subjects. Her books include *Franz Reznicek. Bauten und Projekte der Moderne*, Innsbruck 1995; *Das Maß im Kochen*, Innsbruck 1999; *Die Entwicklung der Küche in der Architektur*, in: *Brennpunkt Küche: planen, ausstatten, nutzen*, Feldkirch 2001; *eigen + sinnig. Der Werkraum Bregenzerwald als Modell für ein neues Handwerk*, Munich 2005.

Gion Caminada, b. 1957 in Vrin, Switzerland. Trained as a joiner; attended the school of applied arts; post-diploma architectural studies at ETH Zurich; own architecture practice in Vrin; assistant professor and lecturer in architecture and design at ETH Zurich since 1998; numerous buildings especially in Vrin including a room for the bodies of the departed, stables, community buildings, homes; various commendations including a commendation for good buildings in the canton of Grisons in 1994 and 2001 and the international *Sexten Kultur* architecture prize in 2006; exhibitions include *Cul zuffel e l'aura dado* in the Kunsthaus Chur in 2006.

Peter Davey, b. 1940 in Cleckheaton, Yorkshire. Architectural critic and historian; from 1980 to 2005 editor, *The Architectural Review*, London. Publications include *Architecture of the Arts and Crafts Movement*, 1980; *Heikkinen & Komonen*, 1994; *Arts and Crafts Architecture*, 1995; *Peter Zumthor*, 1998; numerous contributions to international architectural publications.

Barbara Ettinger-Brinckmann, b. 1950 in Oberbruch-Grebben, Germany. Architect; from 1974 to 1975 academic assistant at town planning institute of the University of Stuttgart; from 1975 to 1977 freelance academic post at the Gesamthochschule Kassel, worked in the city of Kassel's monument preservation department; from 1977 to 1980 worked in the *Büro für Bedarfsplanung/Arbeitsgruppe Nutzungsforschung*, Kassel; freelance architect since 1980, from 1980 to 1992 partner in the demand planning office/user research working group with Prof. Peter Jokusch and Manfred Hegger (until 1989), Kassel; from 1993 ANP – *Architektur und Nutzungsplanung* (architecture and functional planning) practice in Kassel, partnership with Michael Bergholter since 1994; from 1997 to 2002 chair of the BDA group in Kassel, member of the BDA Land managing committee; initiator and from 1998 chair of the Kassel Architekturzentrum in the Kulturbahnhof; from 2000 to 2004 vice-president of the Hesse Chamber of Architects and Town Planners; president of the Hesse Chamber of Architects and Town Planners since 2004.

Onno Faller, b. 1965 in Karlsruhe, Germany. Studied "Film and cooking as an art genre" under Professor Peter Kubelka, *Hochschule für Bildende Künste Städelschule* Frankfurt am Main from 1989 to 1995; freelance food curator and cook from 2001; from 1999 to 2001 taught at the *Städelschule* and directed the cookery workshop; has taught cooking as an art genre at the technical college Mainz, the *Hochschule für Gestaltung und Kunst* in Zurich in 2003, the Jan van Eyck Academy Maastricht in 2003/2004; founded the "cookery workshop" for cooking as an art genre in 2002; since then numerous lectures, exhibitions and cookery events, research work and seminars on the subject of cooking as an art genre.

Annette Gigon, b. 1959 in Herisau, Switzerland. Diploma at the ETH Zurich in 1984; worked in various architecture practices from 1984 to 1989, also own practice from 1987 to 1989; joint practice with Mike Guyer since 1989; visiting lecturer at the EPF Lausanne from 2001 to 2002; numerous buildings including: Kirchner Museum Davos; extension for the art museum in Winterthur; extension and renovation for the Sammlung Oskar Reinhart, Winterthur; Museum Carl Liner, Appenzell; Archaeological Museum and Park in Bramsche-Kalkriese Osnabrück; Museum Albers/Honegger, Mouans-Sartoux, France; current projects include: conversion for the *Kunstmuseum Basel*, Laurenzbau; high-rise office block Prime-Tower, Zurich; new buildings for the *Verkehrshaus der Schweiz*, Lucerne; numerous contributions to exhibitions and also individual exhibitions: *Werkstoff* in the architectural gallery Lucerne 1993, *gebaut nicht gebaut* in *the architektur forum Zürich*, December 2004 – February 2005; numerous prizes including *Fritz-Schumacher-Preis* from the Alfred Toepfer Stiftung 2002; important publications on Gigon/Guyer Architekten: Gigon Guyer Architekten / Arbeiten 1989 - 2000, Sulgen 2000, Annette Gigon Mike Guyer 1989-2000, Madrid 2000.

Andreas Hartmann, b. 1952 in Freiburg im Breisgau, Germany. Professor of folklore/European ethnology at the University of Münster from 1998; doctorate 1984 with a thesis on *Freiburg im Breisgau around 1900. Urban self-confidence at the turn of the 20th century*, post-doctoral thesis 1998, a work of academic history on the relationship between cultural research and the analysis of memory. As well as a large number of works on different subjects relating to the history of culture and ideas he has published various empirical studies including *Grenzgeschichten. Berichte aus dem deutschen Niemandsland* (with Sabine Künsting 1990) and *Zungenglück und Gaumenqualen. Geschmackserinnerungen* 1994; for some years he has specialised additionally in socio-cosmological exchange processes in the age of globalisation; research and development for the Living Silk project in North-East Thailand.

Petra Hagen Hodgson, b. 1957 in Palo Alto, CA, USA. Grew up in Varese, Italy; studied German literature and art history in Zurich; from 1987 to 1990 taught history of architecture at the University of Hong Kong; from 1990 to 1994 teaching assignments at the Hochschule für Gestaltung in Zurich; freelance architecture critic from 1995; numerous publications, books including *Städtebau im Kreuzverhör. Max Frisch zum Städtebau der fünfziger Jahre*, Baden 1986; correspondent for the Swiss architecture magazine *Werk, Bauen und Wohnen*, architectural photographer; public relations; advisor to the Academy of the Hesse Chamber of Architects and Town Planners from 2000; devises and leads international symposia.

Wilhelm Klauser, b. 1961 in Stuttgart, Germany. Studied architecture in Stuttgart and Paris; doctorate in Berlin; from 1992 to 1998 working in the field of architecture and urbanism as author and curator in Tokyo, then in Paris until 2003; since then in Berlin; architect and author; publications on architecture and cities at home and abroad; has taught in different countries including Japan, France and Germany; 2003 founded InitialDesign – InD; works in Berlin and Paris.

153

Peter Kubelka, b. 1934 in Vienna, Austria. Artist and theoretician; works in the field of film, cooking, music, architecture; communication of a world view that does not depend on words through events with examples based on seeing, hearing, feeling, tasting; studied music; avant-garde film-maker since 1952; metric films from 1957; co-founder and director of the *Österreichisches Filmmuseum* in 1964; film *Unsere Afrikareise* 1966; has taught in the USA since 1966; co-founder of the Anthology Filmarchives in New York in 1970; designed and realised an ideal cinema: *The Invisible Cinema*; started theoretical work on cooking; at the *Hochschule für Bildende Künste Städelschule* in Frankfurt am Main since 1978, where for the first time at an art college cooking has been recognised and taught as a fully valid artistic discipline since 1980; professor of "Film and Cooking as an Art Genre" at the *Städelschule* from 1979 to 1999. Since then events world-wide including all cultural phenomena holistically.

Stanislaus von Moos, b. 1940 in Lucerne, Switzerland. Art historian; professor of modern art at the University of Zurich from 1983 to 2005; has taught at the Accademia di architettura, in Mendrisio, Switzerland, since 2005; author of numerous books including: *Le Corbusier, Elemente einer Synthese*, Frauenfeld 1968 and Cambridge, MA 1978ff; *Turm und Bollwerk*, Zurich 1974; Venturi, *Scott Brown & Associates. Buildings and Projects*, New York, Munich 1987, 2nd vol. New York 1999; *Industrieästhetik*, Disentis 1992; *Fernand Léger: La Ville. Zeitdruck, Großstadt, Wahrnehmung*, Frankfurt am Main 1999; *Le Corbusier Before Le Corbusier* (ed. with Arthur Rüegg), New Haven/London 2001; *Nicht Disneyland. Aufsätze über Modernität und Nostalgie*, Zurich 2004.

Ákos Moravánszky, b. 1950 in Székesfehérvár, Hungary. Professor of architectural theory at the ETH Zurich since 1996; from 1989 to 1991 research associate at the Getty Center for the History of Art and the Humanities in Santa Monica and from 1991 to 1996 visiting professor at the Massachusetts Institute of Technology; from 2003 to 2004 visiting professor at the University of Applied Art in Budapest as Szent-Györgyi Fellow; his numerous books include *Die Erneuerung der Baukunst: Wege zur Moderne in Mitteleuropa*, Salzburg 1988; *Competing Visions: Aesthetic Invention and Social Imagination in Central European Architecture, 1867-1918*, Cambridge, Mass. 1998; *Räumlinge: Valentin Bearth & Andrea Deplazes*, Lucerne 1999; *Architekturtheorie im 20. Jahrhundert: Eine kritische Anthologie*, Vienna/New York 2003.

154

Paul von Naredi-Rainer, b. 1950 in Knittelfeld, Austria. Full professor of art history at the University of Innsbruck since 1988; director of the *Rheinisches Bildarchiv (Museen der Stadt Köln)* from 1976 to 1988; his most important books include *Architektur und Harmonie. Zahl, Maß und Proportion in der abendländischen Baukunst*, Cologne 1982, 7th ed. 2001; *Salomos Tempel und das Abendland. Monumentale Folgen historischer Irrtümer*, Cologne 1994; *Museum Buildings. A Design Manual*, Basel, Berlin, Boston 2004.

Fritz Neumeyer, b. 1946 in Bahrdorf, Germany. Professor of architectural theory at the Technical University, Berlin since 1993; John Labatoot professor for Architecture and Urbanism, Princeton University in 1992; professor of building history at the University of Dortmund from 1989 to 1992; visiting professorships at the Southern California Institute of Architecture, Santa Monica, the Graduate School of Design, Harvard University, in the architecture faculty of the University of Leuven, at the Institut d'Humanitats de Barcelona and the Universidad de Navarra, Pamplona; from 1988 to 1989 Research Fellow at the Getty Center for the History of Arts and the Humanities, Santa Monica; his most important book publications include: *Mies van der Rohe. Das kunstlose Wort*, Berlin 1986; *Friedrich Gilly 1772-1800. Essays on Architecture*, Santa Monica 1994; *Der Klang der Steine. Nietzsches Architekturen*, Berlin 2001; Quellentexte zur Architekturtheorie, Munich 2002.

Carlo Petrini, b. 1949 in Bra, Piedmont, Italy. Journalist; lives and works in Bra; founder and president of the international Slow Food movement; organiser and patron of numerous gastronomic events like *Cheese, Salone del Gusto or Terra Madre*; publisher for *Slow Food Editore*, which made its name with books like *Vini d'Italia*; other books published by different houses like *Le ragioni del gusto*, Laterza 2001; *Buono, pulito e giusto. Principi di nuova gastronomia*, Enaudi 2005; supports producers in developing countries; initiator of the first good taste college, the *Università del gusto*; numerous prizes for journalistic activities including for the magazine *Slow, Messaggero di Gusto e Cultura*, the *Utne Reader Alternative Press Award 2001*, the Australian *Jacob's Creek Gold Ladle* prize 2003; won the International Wine and Spirit Competition *Communicator of the Year Trophy* in 2000, the *Premio Sicco Mansholt* for a new sustainable agriculture model; honorary doctorate in cultural anthropology from the University *Istituto Universitario Suor Orsola Benincasa* in Naples in 2003; *Eckart Witzigmann Preis* from the *Deutsche Akademie für Kulinaristik* in 2004.

Udo Pollmer, b. 1954 in Himmelpforten, Germany. Food scientist, journalist and corporate consultant. From 1991 to 1999 taught at the technical college in Fulda; since 1995 scientific director of the European Institute for Food and Nutritional Sciences. (EU.L.E.); numerous publications in the print media, radio and TV broadcasts; books include: *Iß und stirb – Chemie in unserer Nahrung*, Cologne 1982 (with E. Kapfelsperger); *Prost Mahlzeit – Krank durch gesunde Ernährung*, Cologne 1994 (with A. Fock, U. Gonder, K. Haug); *Liebe geht durch die Nase – Was unser Verhalten beeinflusst und lenkt*, Cologne 1997 (with A. Fock, U. Gonder, K. Haug); *Lexikon der populären Ernährungsirrtümer*, Frankfurt am Main 2001 (with S. Warmuth); *Lexikon der Fitness-Irrtümer*, Frankfurt am Main 2003 (with G. Frank, S. Warmuth); *Esst endlich normal!*, Munich 2005; *Food Design: Panschen erlaubt*, Stuttgart 2006 (with M. Niehaus).

Ian Ritchie, b. 1947 in Hove, Great Britain. Director of Ian Ritchie Architects Ltd and co-founded Rice Francis Ritchie (RFR) design engineers, Paris; these practices have realised and contributed to major new works throughout Europe, including the Reina Sofia Museum of Modern Art in Madrid, the Leipzig Glass Hall, the Louvre Sculpture Courts and Pyramids and La Villette Cité des Sciences in Paris, the Jubilee Line Extension and International Regatta Centre in London, The Spire in Dublin and the RSC Courtyard Theatre; visiting Professor of architecture in Moscow, Vienna and Leeds School of Civil Engineering, taught at the Architectural Association, Royal Academy of Arts Professor of Architecture, London; publications: *Connected Architecture*, Ian Ritchie, Berlin/London 1994; *The biggest glass palace in the world*, Ian Ritchie & Ingerid Helsing Almaas, New York 1997; Alessandro Rocca: *Ian Ritchie, Technoecologia*, Milano 1998; *Plymouth Theatre Royal Production Centre*, London 2003; *The Spire* London 2004; *The RSC Courtyard Theatre* London 2006, *The Leipzig Book of Drawings* London 2006; many national and international prizes and exhibitions.

Claudio Silvestrin, b. 1954 in Zurich. Educated in Milan by his master A.G. Fronzoni and studied in London at the Architectural Association; since 1989 he has been practicing worldwide from his London office known as Claudio Silvestrin architects; work encompasses day-to-day objects, domestic and commercial interiors, art galleries and museums, newly built houses for private residence and for real estate development; Claudio Silvestrin Architects is currently in the process to design a new 40,000 m² construction resort in Ceará, Brazil to include a new hotel, spa and villas; clients include Giorgio Armani, illycaffé, Anish Kapoor, Calvin Klein, Poltrona Frau, Fondazione Sandretto Re Rebaudengo, Kanye West; publication: Franco Bertoni *Claudio Silvestrin* Basel 1999.

Rolf Toyka, b. 1950 in Krefeld, Germany. Dipl.-Ing. Architect; studied architecture at the TU Braunschweig and the ETH Zurich; worked as an architect in various practices; municipal architect in Geesthacht near Hamburg for five years; taught in the architecture/interior design department at various higher education institutions (eight years in all); director of the *Academy of the Hesse Chamber of Architects and Town Planners* since 1987; editor and author of numerous books; worked on various advisory boards, including the City of Wiesbaden's urban development and architecture advisory board.

Illustration Credits

Rolf Toyka/Barbara Ettinger-Brinckmann: Foreword
p. 6 Petra Hagen Hodgson, in Harald Wohlfahrt's kitchen
p. 7 Jean-Luc Valentin, Jo Franzke's architecture practice

Petra Hagen Hodgson: Introduction
All illustrations: Petra Hagen Hodgson

Peter Kubelka: Architecture and Food Composition
p. 16 VG Bild-Kunst, Bonn 2006, photograph: Petra Hagen Hodgson
All others: Petra Hagen Hodgson

Paul von Naredi-Rainer: Measurement and Number in Architecture
p. 23 (c) FLC/VG Bild-Kunst, Bonn 2006
All others: author's archives

Renate Breuß: Measurements in Cooking
p. 30 60.215 - bpk Bildarchiv Preußischer Kulturbesitz/Scala
p. 31 Bruno Klomfar
p. 32 Kunstgeschichtliches Institut, University of Frankfurt am Main
p. 35 Petra Hagen Hodgson
p. 37 Archive of the Hesse Chamber of Architects and Town Planners, from: C.H. Baer: Moderne Bauformen. Monatshefte für Architektur und Raumkunst. Stuttgart 1919

Materials and Colours. Annette Gigon in Conversation with Petra Hagen Hodgson
p. 38, 40, 42, 44, 45 Heinrich Helfenstein
p. 39 Arazebra Fotographie Helbling & Kupferschmid
p. 41 top and bottom right: Petra Hagen Hodgson; bottom left: Gaston Wicky
p. 43 top Heinrich Helfenstein; bottom Harald F. Müller
p. 46, 47 Petra Hagen Hodgson
p. 49 Serge Demailly

Fritz Neumeyer: Hearth and Home
p. 57 author's archive
p. 58 51.483 – bpk Bildarchiv Preußischer Kulturbesitz/Paris, Musée d'Orsay/RMN/photograph: Gerard Le Gall/Hervé Lewandowski
All others: Petra Hagen Hodgson

Stanislaus von Moos: Rules of Fasting and Desire Derailed
pp. 63-65 FLC/VG Bild-Kunst, Bonn 2006, models, based on author's archives
p. 69 Venturi Scott Brown and Associates
p. 71 Stefan Müller
All others: author's archives

Ákos Moravánszky: The Reproducibility of Taste
p. 72 Nicolas Hodgson
p. 70 Siemens AG
p. 78 Stuttgarter Gesellschaft für Kunst und Denkmalpflege e.V., photograph: Franz J. Much
p. 81 Nicolas Hodgson
All others: author's archives

Gion Caminada: Meaningful Architecture in a Globalised World
All illustrations: Lucia Degonda

Andreas Hartmann: The Eater and his Ancestors
p. 97 Alinari 2006/Artothek
All others: author's archives

The AT 400 table ventilation. A sculpture
on the worktop. A revolution in recirculation
technology. Restaurant-grade performance
for the home chef: highly efficient extraction
right where vapours occur. Integrated lighting
perfectly illuminates the cooking area.
Additional workspace to prepare and serve.
Perfect for an island solution in your kitchen.
Ask our partners and friends.
www.gaggenau.com
The difference is Gaggenau.

GAGGENAU